PRAISE FOR
SHOW YOUR WORTH

Show Your Worth is for all aspiring leaders who are in search of uncovering and discovering their superpower by being their authentic selves, emerging as successful leaders on their own terms.

It is a practical, actionable, and thoughtful guide with intentional strategies by the inspirational leader Shelmina Babai Abji, who has been there, who knows the struggle firsthand and has defied the odds, as well as defying that voice in your head that says "You're not good enough" or questions "Do you really belong?"

Shelmina is a true role model for every female leader in tech to look up to; her story will inspire millions of women out there to emerge as global leaders.

—**ANNA RADULOVSKI**, founder and CEO,
WomenTech Network

Shelmina Babai Abji has written a compelling, comprehensive, and easy-to-understand guide for how women can use the power of strategic intent to show their worth. She clearly lays out eight strategies that all career women can utilize to better themselves and emerge as strong leaders. You will relate to her stories and those of other inspiring women who share their journeys. Best of all, Shelmina gives you exercises to do in each chapter so that you can immediately apply the insights from this book. As an educator, I want all female graduates who aspire to become leaders to read this treasure!

—**SAMINA KARIM**, PhD, Professor of Strategy &
Innovation, Northeastern University

As a fellow apprentice, a corporate sister, and a soulmate, Shelmina has always been a guiding light and conscience for me and others whose lives she has touched with generosity, passion, and care.

There is no preservation or hesitation in Shelmina's way of living. She pours her heart and mind into everything she does, be it family, career, friendship, love, worldly cause, or a book of revelation and precious learning—that book being the one in your hands.

As you read these pages, I trust that you will feel her passion, her conviction, and most importantly her presence. Shelmina shares intimately, dearly, and wholeheartedly.

Shelmina, thank you for being who you are and thank you for sharing your life with us.

—ZARINA LAM STANFORD, Chief Marketing
Officer, Bazaarvoice

Reading this book is like having a C-suite mentor all to yourself. Filled with practical advice and inspiring stories, *Show Your Worth* will teach you how to discern what is most worthy of your attention, and empower you to move forward with purpose. Shelmina has written the ultimate guidebook for ambitious women who want to grow their lives as well as their careers.

—REBECCA WEAVER, CEO, HRuprise

In *Show Your Worth*, Shelmina weaves inspirational stories including her own life story with valuable insights and tangible guidance for women. It reveals what I believe to be a step-by-step guide to how to approach your career with intention, no matter where you are in that journey. The wisdom in this book is relevant for women across the globe and comes from a female executive who has practiced it and now has put it into real-life terms for all of us.

—SABINA JOSEPH, General Manager,
Amazon Web Services

In a society where we are bombarded with leadership development advice, what we need are genuine stories of life experiences and lessons learned, told by those who have a sincere desire to lift women up. Shelmina and this book do just that. Ask yourself these four questions, and if you uncover the truth, your star will rise: What do I believe? What do I want? What brings me joy? Who am I?

> —**SUSAN ROCCO**, founder and host of Women to Watch Media®

As an engineering manager in technology, a single mom, an immigrant, and a woman of color, Shelmina provides guidance that will help me scale new heights. If I had this book early in my career, it would have been a game changer.

> —**KAVITA RYALI**, Principal Program Manager, Microsoft

As a Korean American recent college graduate, I stumble through the vast choices of possibilities and opportunities and grapple with the constant question: How do I succeed at work and life?

For me, *Show Your Worth* is a guide that answers my many questions and provides concrete direction on how I can achieve success. It has the advice I need to navigate the complexities of my career. This book will be my lifelong companion providing me with camaraderie, mentorship, motivation, and confidence at every step of my journey as a career woman aspiring to emerge as a leader.

> —**CHRISTINE KIM**, Sales, Operations, and Planning, SK Hynix America

Whether you are working from home, hybrid, or in the office, Shelmina's guidance around being intentional with your attention and not getting caught up in a task trap and to-do lists is invaluable. It also releases fear and guilt in the process. An empowering read for anyone wanting to win at work and life.

—**Nikki Bush**, CSP, Hall of Fame Speaker and
author of *Future-Proof Yourself*

Shelmina is one of the few women leaders I know who give very practical advice while encouraging girls to dream big. It's that balance in her, where she walks the earth but thinks the sky is her limit and works toward it, that I have always cherished.

She has guided me, and many other women and girls, to go for the biggest achievements possible while always reminding me to have a very sound plan to walk the talk.

I consider it our good fortune that she has taken the time to write this book and pass so much on to the next generation of young women, to help them achieve their highest potential.

—**Purvi Gandhi**, early- and growth-stage
technology investor, Silicon Valley

Shelmina Abji's book, *Show Your Worth*, is filled with practical advice for women who are early professionals, in their mid-career, or even experienced professionals like myself. I was most touched by the programming analogy that Shelmina shares while she mentors an early professional woman who is trying to build her confidence to speak up in team meetings. There are many words of wisdom in this book such as "focus on progress, not perfection," which is relevant advice for all women in general. While we currently live in a more agile, flex-working world with a different set of tools than Shelmina talks about, her advice and tips are as relevant here too. This is a book that I would like to always have on my table as a ready reference. It's a book that I will gift to my young professional daughter to use as a guiding reference to success, and it will always be a book that I hope my granddaughters will read when they enter the workforce of the future!

—**Radha Ratnaparkhi**, VP and CTO,
T. J. Watson Research Center, IBM

Shelmina draws on her unique experiences, her impressive career accomplishments, and a strong sense of purpose and intentionality to create a compelling blueprint for women looking to advance their own careers. Her fierce advocacy and commitment to women business leaders is as inspirational as the trail she's blazed in her own life. *Show Your Worth* is an incredible resource—whether you're just starting out in the working world or a seasoned veteran.

—**Chris Nassetta**, CEO, Hilton

In *Show Your Worth*, Shelmina beautifully shares a blueprint for how women can emerge as leaders in their fields. From showcasing the importance of women supporting other women to digging deep in difficult times, Shelmina's own story of empowerment and the powerful insights she's learned along the way can help inspire a new generation of female leaders.

—**Stephanie Linnartz**, President,
Marriott International

The framework Shelmina lays out in *Show Your Worth* helps women navigate the all-too-common career challenges and pitfalls we have all faced. This book should be in every woman's hand to ensure we close the gender gap in corporate America.

—**Deidra Merriwether**, Chief Financial
Officer, W.W. Grainger

Energizing. Gritty. Powerful. Refreshing. Inspirational. This is the kind of book you put down and feel empowered and equipped to get out there (right away!) and conquer. Through presenting her own life's experience with grace, confidence, humility, and passion, Shelmina has shown that all women, and especially women of color, can reach great heights both professionally and personally while overcoming significant challenges and has provided a very practical guide for anyone aspiring to do so. A must-read not only for women, but for all underrepresented minorities to incorporate in their journey to success.

—**SHAMSAH FATIMA DHALA**, Principal
Investment Officer, The World Bank Group

Show Your Worth provides the reader an opportunity to take a walk with Shelmina and other powerful women leaders like her and learn about their experiences being a leader in corporate America. I loved how the book defines practical ways in which you can approach your career and how to balance it with the realities of life. This will be a game changer for women in the business world, especially as we emerge from the post-pandemic environment.

—**ASHA VARGHESE**, President,
Caterpillar Foundation

The hike to success is more of a journey through a distracting maze than an upward climb. The destination is constantly shifting, as we gain insight, skill, and experience. Without intention, wisdom of self, honest internal check-ins, and the ability to prioritize smartly, you can still arrive at a destination and feel cheated. I think this is one fear or realization many of us share—getting "there" and feeling disappointed. *Show Your Worth* shows you how to redraw the map at every stage and which tools you need to get to the "there" where the heart feels at home, the mind at ease, and the spirit in flow.

I've known Shelmina for years and have always felt drawn to her kindness, her genuine curiosity, and the generosity with which she shares her wisdom. Now that I've read *Show Your Worth*, I feel an eternity of gratitude toward her. I had never experienced a clearer set of definitions, tasks, and motivators to set myself up for the different successes that every phase of life can bring. Shelmina's writing is inviting, her stories are fascinating, and the steps and processes she describes are universal, yet nuanced. I've already filled pages with introspection and to-dos while reading this book. I've reset my goals and priorities in ways that make the journey energizing rather than overwhelming. I wish I had this guide all along the way, but I'm thankful it will accompany me on the road ahead.

—LILIA LUCIANO, correspondent at CBS News

I loved this book! Shelmina Abji is so inspiring to me, and she did a fantastic job of turning her trials and tribulations into lessons to help others so they don't have to go through the same challenges. This book would have served me well earlier in my career as much as it has helped me as a CFO today. *Show Your Worth* is a wonderful gift to all readers. Shelmina certainly pays it forward, and this book will have the multiplier effect.

—ZAHRA HIRANI, CFO, Boeing Capital Corporation

SHOW
YOUR WORTH

SHOW YOUR WORTH

8 INTENTIONAL STRATEGIES FOR WOMEN TO EMERGE AS LEADERS AT WORK

SHELMINA BABAI ABJI

NEW YORK   CHICAGO   SAN FRANCISCO   ATHENS   LONDON
MADRID   MEXICO CITY   MILAN   NEW DELHI
SINGAPORE   SYDNEY   TORONTO

1 2 3 4 5 6 7 8 9   LCR   27 26 25 24 23 22

ISBN   978-1-264-26924-2
MHID   1-264-26924-2

e-ISBN   978-1-264-26925-9
e-MHID   1-264-26925-0

Design by Mauna Eichner and Lee Fukui

McGraw Hill books are available at special quantity discounts to use as premiums and sales promotions or for use in corporate training programs. To contact a representative, please visit the Contact Us pages at www.mhprofessional.com.

McGraw Hill is committed to making our products accessible to all learners. To learn more about the available support and accommodations we offer, please contact us at accessibility@mheducation.com. We also participate in the Access Text Network (www.accesstext.org), and ATN members may submit requests through ATN.

This book is dedicated to my late Mom who worked tirelessly to raise my three siblings and me. She was my first inspiration to succeed. Spending her last few weeks with her inspired me to make others successful and leave behind a legacy.

CONTENTS

FOREWORD

We are all mere mortals in real time,
but with the benefit of hindsight
we become geniuses.
RODNEY ADKINS

LEADERS ARE not born; instead, they grow out of a lifetime of experiences. My earliest memory of leadership comes from when I was a young kid and would create secret missions, missions that typically involved disassembling various household appliances. By the time I was 13 years old, all of this came to a reckoning, because my missions started to fall apart. After I disassembled and reassembled a few of our more advanced appliances, some of them did not perform the way they should have. I came from a family who was very disciplined, with strong values, and who barely got by financially, so these missions created unexpected and arguably avoidable expenses and problems. My questionable undertakings finally led to a major inflection point in my life with my parents. I was expecting to be reprimanded in unimaginable ways, but instead, my parents focused on channeling my curiosity in more productive ways. I ended up taking on odd neighborhood jobs to help support my missions. I used the money, along with my allowance, to make purchases at a nearby hobby shop, and the missions grew in complexity and creativity, evolving over time.

Those missions were integral to my preparation in leadership. Through them, I learned an absolutely essential lesson for success in leadership: Curiosity redefines the limits. Great leaders continue to develop and advance because they stay intellectually curious. They commit to lifelong learning in order to remain competitive and relevant.

Fast-forward to my 33-year career at IBM, where I have had the opportunity to meet many knowledgeable people and some amazing leaders from various disciplines. We would refer to some of these leaders as "our best and brightest" because they were second to no one when compared with others in the industry. I remember meeting an up-and-coming competitive account sales leader who was anything but bashful from our West region in 1995 named Shelmina. She came across as extremely purpose-driven by the way she would ask questions and the way she would process her responses. Every time I had the opportunity to engage with Shelmina, I was intrigued by what appeared to be endless curiosity on how to improve her game. She was a sponge for knowledge, and it was evident by how she listened to others who she felt had something to offer.

As I watched Shelmina's development and growth, I discovered that she possessed some of the greatest characteristics found in a true leader. She was curious, she listened, she truly cared about people, and people wanted to be associated with her. As a leader, she always came across as working for the people versus thinking people were working for her. I knew with absolute certainty that she was a rising star. She was very in tune with the market landscape as well as her customers. Over the years, she was recognized as a top seller at IBM Golden Circle events. In addition, I had the opportunity to recognize her for winning new IBM customers and winning back previous IBM customers at my annual global group business events.

In July 2002, I was fortunate enough to be in a senior leadership position where I could appoint a next-generation leader to a position we called an executive assistant (EA). This was a practice in IBM that was a combination of recognition, development, and potentially advancement at the conclusion of the one-year assignment. The EA was assigned specific projects and tasks during the appointment; however, the greatest value was getting a glimpse into the daily operations and the role of a senior executive. During my tenure, I have had the opportunity to work with a number of up-and-coming leaders, but the competitive accounts sales leader from our West region whom I met in 1995 became one of my best appointments. As her mentor, I benefited just as much from our relationship as she did, because she was a perfect example of reverse mentoring. Because of my perpetual need to stay intellectually curious, her insights and points of view served to support me in being more effective as a senior leader in the industry.

It has been a privilege to be a part of Shelmina's continued journey since meeting her in 1995 and watching her evolve as a great leader and a great human being. It is my honor to introduce *Show Your Worth*, a powerful map with which to navigate your leadership journey led by your invaluable guide, Shelmina Babai Abji.

—RODNEY ADKINS

ACKNOWLEDGMENTS

AMONG THE many people who inspired me to write this book, I must first thank all the women who trusted me with their struggles at work and gave me the honor to guide them toward success.

I also want to thank the thousands of women who, after hearing me speak, have taken the time to speak with me and asked if I have written a book.

Much gratitude to all the women who invited me to speak at their corporations, conferences, and universities. You provided me with a tremendous platform to engage with thousands of women globally, which gave me the proof that my insights worked not only for me, but for career women globally.

You have all inspired me to extend my sphere of influence and reach even more career women throughout the world.

Rodney Adkins for not only being an incredible mentor, sponsor, and a role model leader, but also for taking time out of his very busy schedule to write the Foreword of my book.

Susan Whitney for seeing potential in me when I was content with small successes. Thank you for being my mentor and role model leader. You made me feel special every time I interacted with you, and I can't thank you enough for that.

Claudith Washington and Patricia Duarte for their support to obtain my green card.

Keith Elzia for being the best sales leader one could ask for. Your coaching set me up for success not just in sales but also in life.

Thank you to all my teachers in my career and my life: my parents, children, siblings, extended family and friends, my mentors, bosses, peers, sponsors. I consider myself very fortunate to have you all in my life.

This book would not have been possible without the support of many other women as well:

Sangeeta Singh-Kurtz for editing the first draft of my book proposal and providing invaluable feedback, and Michele Matrisciani for helping me craft and edit my book proposal while also loving the subject matter.

Marilyn Allen, my literary agent, for not only believing in me and representing my work but also providing her invaluable guidance throughout the entire process.

My daughter, Sophia Babai, who helped me better understand the difference between writing and speaking.

My team of editors including Sophia Babai, Alexis Gargagliano, and Alessandra Lusardi for helping me finalize my book manuscript.

My editor at McGraw Hill, Cheryl Segura, for improving my book, asking questions that are nothing short of genius, and having patience with me as I worked hard to create maximum value for my readers.

I would like to thank my project manager Patricia Wallenburg for her attention to detail and her kind demeanor.

Munira Rahemtulla for reading my manuscript and not only editing my book but also providing tremendous feedback for improvement.

Profound thanks to my alma mater, University of Wisconsin–La Crosse for inviting me as a keynote speaker for their conference, Women Moving Ahead, on April 17, 2015. That was the day I knew my insights could help other career women. That was the day I became an empowerment speaker.

Thank you to all the young women who inspire me with your

dedication to gender equality through my board work at Girl Up and Young Women Empowered.

Thank you to the eight women I deeply respect and admire for sharing their inspiring stories in this book: Vernā Myers, Johanna Maska, Priscilla Eun-Young Abji, Kathleen Hogan, Melissa Kilby, Jennifer DaSilva, Gwendolyn Sykes, and Erica Qualls-Battey.

I want to thank everyone that took time out of their very busy schedules to read my book and provide testimonials: Nikki Bush, Shamsah Fatima Dhala, Purvi Gandhi, Zahra Hirani, Sabina Joseph, Samina Karim, Christine Kim, Stephanie Linnartz, Lilia Luciano, Deidra Merriwether, Chris Nassetta, Radha Ratnaparkhi, Susan Rocco, Anna Rudolawski, Kavita Ryali, Zarina Lam Stanford, Asha Varghese, and Rebecca Weaver.

I also want to thank the countless number of women who are focused on lifting other women—you inspire me every day.

Lastly, I want to thank my husband, Minaz Abji, and my son, Samir Babai, for their unwavering love and support in doing the extra work around the house while I was consumed with writing this book.

INTRODUCTION

WE OFTEN talk about the "glass ceiling" that prevents women from reaching senior leadership positions. But the reality is that women are thwarted much earlier in their attempt to climb the ladder to the top—there's a broken rung far down the ladder that's keeping them from taking that first step up to manager. Fixing this broken rung is the key to achieving parity. This broken-rung inequality surfaces early in our careers and compounds at each subsequent level. At the highest levels, less than 10 percent of leaders are women, and for women of color, like me, the numbers are even smaller.

You, with your aspiration and resolve to become a leader, combined with my insights, will become the change to create gender parity in leadership roles at all levels.

WHY ME?

When I was a little girl, growing up in Mwanza, Tanzania, my toys were old soda bottles and kitchen utensils, and most of my clothes were hand-me-downs. I'd never heard the term "senior executive," and the United States was a rich, faraway land that might as well have existed in a fairy tale. My mother, who had a fourth-grade education, got married at the age of 14 and had her first child at the age of 15. She cooked for others and sold food on the streets to make money to raise her four children. Watching my parents struggle for money, I was determined to obtain a college degree and lift us out of poverty—despite the fact that there was no education past tenth grade in Mwanza.

I came to the United States to pursue a degree in computer science from the University of Wisconsin–La Crosse, and when I started my career, I was an underrepresented woman in the male-dominated field of technology. I was also undereducated compared to others, underprivileged in my economic status, and underproficient in the language and culture. I now refer to this negative mental chatter as my "unders." The worst part of these unders was that they caused me to think and act "under": undermining myself, undervaluing my opinion, and underestimating my worth.

After many trials and errors, slowly but surely I recognized that though my beginnings were very different from those of my peers and superiors, and no one looked like me, I had my own worth to bring to my workplace. This recognition was critical for me to begin showing my worth.

I gained many insights in my career journey, which helped me go from being the first college graduate in my family to one of the highest-ranking women of color, a senior executive, and a vice president at IBM, a large global technology company. And I achieved this while raising my two children, Sophia and Samir, as a single mother since the time they were, respectively, four and two.

At the peak of my career, I left corporate life to do what I still do today—mentor and speak to thousands of career women around the globe to help them show their worth and emerge as leaders. I do this because I recognize that they too are facing the same internal and external barriers that I did.

They too are discouraged by not seeing enough people in the room who look like them, who are relatable to their race, sex, education level, or cultural and socioeconomic backgrounds.

Many decision makers and influencers tend to promote those with backgrounds, experiences, and characteristics similar to theirs.

Women often get overlooked because of differences in race, gender, socioeconomic, cultural, academic backgrounds, or because they don't see other women in leadership roles within and outside their companies. The reality is that because you're a woman, you'll be perceived differently. This, of course, has nothing to do with you, but is instead a consequence of the unconscious gender biases and negative stereotypes that permeate our workplace culture.

Negative stereotypes and biases are breaking the confidence of many women I work with. I'll show you how you can challenge and change such biases in the chapters ahead.

At meetings, after my keynote addresses and one-on-one sessions that strategize around the barriers that deter women in the workforce, the questions I'm asked are mostly the same. They reveal to me just how confused many career women are about what success truly means and how to achieve it. Women have been taught the tired tropes of *what* to do to become successful. We've all heard them: Face your fears; find your voice; act with confidence; create value; master work-life balance; take a seat at the table; find mentors and sponsors; build relationships; maximize your productivity; own your power. But still, and no matter which country they live in, women ask me, 100 percent of the time, "But, Shelmina, *how* do I face my fear, find my voice, and create value? *How* do I act confidently? *How* do I navigate biases and negative stereotypes? *How* do I build competence and confidence? *How* do I own my power? *How* can I create work-life balance?"

These women, like you, aspire to emerge as leaders—whether they are in corporate careers, work independently as freelancers, or are stay-at-home mothers starting their own businesses. I've noticed that no matter how different our lives are, the essence of our struggles remains the same. They've inspired me to write this book.

As a single mom, a woman of color, and an immigrant from a family without money or education, I recognize that most career books out there aren't written for me. Nor are they written for my daughter, or for the countless young women I've mentored. Deep in my heart, I believe that my life's journey, with all its challenges and opportunities, was preparing me to write this book.

I've found that propelling oneself fast and furiously out of the gate is often at the expense of using a potent power: the power of strategic intention.

Intention is defined as an "aim or a plan," and in the business world, entering without either is like flying against a strong headwind. You run on autopilot reacting to whatever comes your way and yet don't make significant progress. Everything seems harder, more exhausting, and the odds seem to be stacked against you. When you become intentional and strategic, the way you show up and your behavior will change. You'll make meaningful progress every day toward your desired outcomes.

The good news is that your individual aims as a woman aspiring to leadership have never been more in line with the goals of businesses as a whole. Study after study confirms that diversity in leadership is not only desirable but also smart business. You can seize this opportunity if you diligently and persistently apply the eight intentional strategies in this book. These strategies have worked not only for me but also for many other women I've spoken to and mentored.

HOW THIS BOOK IS LAID OUT

This book consists of eight chapters. Chapter 1 introduces the importance of *intentionally* defining what success means to you and why. It involves a deep *introspection*. Self-knowledge is key to having an internal compass that drives you to have a fulfilling and rewarding career, so take your time with this chapter and go back to it often to make changes as you learn more about yourself.

The subsequent chapters focus on how you can intentionally achieve your definition of success:

- Chapter 2 teaches you how to maximize your achievement by choosing what deserves your *attention*.
- Chapter 3 teaches you how to achieve a *work-life balance*.
- Chapter 4 teaches you how to maximize your *value creation*.
- Chapter 5 teaches you how to maximize your *growth*.
- Chapter 6 teaches you about the importance of and how to build key *relationships*.
- Chapter 7 teaches you how to create a *leadership brand* that will serve you in your pursuit of your success.
- Chapter 8 teaches you how to earn your well-deserved *promotion*.

Each chapter builds upon the other, and the chapters are interdependent. Think of them as links in a chain. For example, when you intentionally focus on value creation (Chapter 4) and intentional growth (Chapter 5), you'll attract mentors and sponsors (Chapter 6). When you have mentors and sponsors and a stellar leadership brand (Chapter 7), you increase your chances of promotion (Chapter 8). So while you could go to a specific chapter to find a solution for a particular challenge you're facing right now, know that an integrated approach of applying all the strategies will yield better outcomes. Be aware that the weakest link can potentially break the chain. For example, if you're great at most strategies but don't build the right relationships or don't have a stellar leadership brand, you'll decrease your chances of success.

Every chapter begins with an overview of what you can expect to learn and a story of how I implemented that specific intentional strategy in my life. I also share a story of success from incredible women I respect and admire so you can have multiple perspectives.

Next, I share Intentional Exercises so you can apply the insights to your career. It's key that you apply these insights and change your behavior, and we'll do this in three steps:

1. *Introspection* to gain self-knowledge and determine your current state
2. *Application* to apply the insights and accelerate your movement toward your success
3. *Reflection and Celebration* so you can learn from your past week, course-correct, and celebrate what you achieved to get energized for the following week

Last, we end every chapter with promises you make to yourself, because no matter what, you're responsible for your own success, and you must promise yourself that you'll pursue your success with all you've got.

YOU HAVE TO DO THE WORK

This book isn't a one-and-done read. To maximize the impact of this book, you must apply the insights and change your behavior. Regardless of what you know, if you don't apply that knowledge and change your behavior, the knowledge itself won't help.

Here are some ways to make sure you get the most out of this book:

- Stop frequently to ask yourself how you can apply the knowledge you've acquired.
- Diligently do the recommended exercises.
- Apply the strategies at every opportunity.
- Keep notes showing how and when you've applied these strategies.

- During the first year of your initial read, review this book every month and notice the progress you've made.
- As you evolve and progress in your career, come back to the pages of this book at least once a year. Not only will you notice how much you've changed, but you also will see deeper truths as you begin your new journey to scale new heights.

Together we'll start creating and executing these strategies. As you execute, reflect, and course-correct, you'll get better until you master the strategies. Start slow and seek progress, not perfection. As you execute each strategy, I urge you to practice self-compassion. You'll probably find it difficult to execute these strategies flawlessly all the time—I know, because even after all these years, I still stumble. Frankly, if you don't stumble, you're not pushing your boundaries enough. So when things don't go as planned, don't reprimand yourself. Congratulate yourself for trying. Over time, you'll get better and better.

With that being said, I need you to make one promise to yourself: No matter how many times you stumble, you must promise yourself to learn from the experience and keep your desire burning to emerge as a leader. Promise that you'll never give up on yourself and drop out of the leadership pipeline. People can't knock you out unless you let them. You must own this fact: *Your success is your own doing.*

LET ME BE YOUR MENTOR

I'm your mentor, your guide, and your champion, but you'll be doing all the work. I'm a woman who's defied the odds, and you can, too.

This work won't be easy, but I know you can do it, because you picked up this book in the first place. I can promise you that the results will be worth the effort, as your career and life will transform. You'll show your worth and emerge as a leader. You'll become a role model for many. Your mere presence will be an inspiration to others. You'll become part of the change we all want to see in this world—not just to fix the broken first rung but also achieve gender parity in leadership roles—at every level.

Are you ready? Let's get started!

INTENTIONAL
SUCCESS

Don't let anyone rob you of your imagination,
your creativity, or your curiosity. It's your place
in the world; it's your life. Go on and do all you
can with it, and make it the life you want to live.

MAE JEMISON,
first Black woman in space

INTENTIONALLY DEFINING what success means to you and *why* is the first of the eight intentional strategies to help you show your worth and emerge as a leader. It's the most important one, as it's your internal compass—it sets the direction you'll follow and influences all your choices.

The fact that you're reading this book makes it clear that you want to emerge as a leader, and that's fantastic. However, it's important that you emerge as a leader on your own terms. This will allow you to keep rising higher and higher while enjoying what you do and living a fulfilling life, all the while keeping your goals and intentions for success in mind.

Success means different things to different people—as it should. Success has plasticity; it is meant to change, expand, grow, and evolve as you do. But if you don't intentionally define it, you won't take the necessary steps to achieve it.

This is your life and your career, and you must decide for yourself what success looks like for you, not what anyone else expects of you. Don't get caught up in other people's expectations of what you're supposed to accomplish.

This doesn't mean that you completely discount the perspectives of others. Feel free to get perspectives from people you trust, respect, and admire, but only keep what resonates with you. Other people may have good advice, but it may not serve *your* dreams.

It's easy to get caught up in others' expectations of what you should accomplish or who you should become, but when the going gets tough, and it will, you'll be tempted to give up if you're pursuing someone else's dream. And even if you achieve someone else's vision of success, it will ring hollow.

INSIGHT

Your success must be on your terms. Don't let anyone define you or your success.

Can you imagine driving to one destination but arriving at another because your GPS was programmed by another person? That's exactly what happens when you allow others to define your success and your *why*.

Let me share my personal story of when I intentionally defined success in my career.

Five years into my career, I was in a room full of women, and still no one looked like me, and I began to wonder, yet again, "Do I even belong in this room?" It was my second year at my second job, and I had won an award for my performance, which included an invitation to a women's roundtable with our Midwest general manager, Susan Whitney. She sat at the head of a shiny, oval mahogany table at the center of a large corporate boardroom. I sat in awe of her along with all the other high achievers in the room. Susan's purple dress, her beautiful diamond earrings, and her grace and intelligence dazzled me.

I had just returned from a recognition trip to San Francisco for the above-mentioned award, the Rookie Systems Engineer of the Year, where I was whisked into a world of luxury far from my one-bedroom apartment in Minneapolis and even farther from my humble home in Tanzania. All the award winners were flown in and treated like royalty. Everything was new to me—I had never eaten sushi before, never drunk fine wine, and certainly never stayed at a five-star hotel. I spent the entire time wondering the same question, "Do I belong here?"

After the women's roundtable, my manager's manager had asked me to accompany Susan back to his office. As we walked down the hallway, Susan smiled at me and said, "Congratulations on winning such a prestigious award, Shelmina."

I was blown away that she knew about the award and shocked that she knew my name. I barely managed to get out, "Thank you."

As casually as one would ask someone's restaurant preference, Susan asked me, "Where do you want to be in five years?"

Five years? I just felt lucky and content to be there in the present. "I . . . I haven't thought that far ahead," I admitted with a glazed look. "I get so focused on doing the best possible job right now that I don't really think about what's next."

"You should," Susan advised. Her firm, steady voice indicated this was a fact, not an opinion. "You're right that it's critical that you need to do the best possible job in your current role, but it's equally important to think about what you want to do next, and next after that. That way, you'll always be working toward something bigger. You've got so much potential."

Her words sparked a firestorm in my brain. "*Me?* So much potential? I could work toward something bigger?"

I felt a flutter in my stomach. It took me back to what I had come to understand was a pivotal moment in my childhood.

I was born into a low-income family in a small town called Mwanza in northwestern Tanzania. I was the third of four siblings, and all of us shared a bedroom. My mother and father completed a fourth-grade and eighth-grade education, respectively, and worked tirelessly to provide for my siblings and me. My mother was married five months after her fourteenth birthday, and six months after her fifteenth birthday, she delivered my oldest sister. Our toys were old soda bottles and kitchen utensils, and most of my clothes were hand-me-downs, but we always had delicious food on the table and a bounty of love and laughter.

My parents had moved to a small mining town called Geita (75 miles from Mwanza) when I was three years old for my dad's job. Two years later, I moved back to Mwanza to start kindergarten, as there were no schools in Geita. I lived with my maternal grandmother, who loved me unconditionally—almost to a fault. I could do nothing wrong in her eyes. At school, my friends and I would be the first ones to run out to play as the bell rang for lunch and after school. I did my homework as quickly as possible without paying any attention to whether I was doing a good job or not. But all that changed in third grade when my parents moved back to Mwanza.

One day, I brought home my report card. It was printed on a thin piece of peach-colored paper, and the grades were handwritten by our teachers—black ink for the better grades: A, B, and C, and red for the poorer grades: Ds and Fs. My report card was riddled with red ink. I ranked 27 out of a class of 30.

My mother stood over a large frying pan, red with the heat that rolled off the burning charcoals as she fried rice cakes, called "vitumbua" in Swahili. She made these to sell around town to supplement my father's income. As soon as she saw my report card, she started crying. Tears rolled down her beautiful red, sweaty face. I loved my mother deeply, and this was not a sight I liked. Confused, I asked her why she was crying. "What did I do wrong?" I wondered.

She responded while sobbing in a very loving and kind way: "I work so hard to educate you, and you failed in every class."

The oil spat and snapped in the pan. Finally, still confused, I said, "You never told me that you wanted me to get good grades."

That was the turning point of my life. I loved my mom so much. It pained me deeply to hurt her, and I promised myself that I'd get good grades to make her happy. She inspired me. I started applying myself and went to school every day with the intention to get good grades to please my mom. I paid more attention in class, while still managing to find time to play, but only after I'd completed all my homework to the best of my ability. My goal was to not have any red on my report card (my simple definition of success) so my mom would be happy (my *why*).

A few months later, report card time rolled around again, and it was customary for the teacher to announce the names of the students that ranked first, second, and third. I never paid attention to these announcements, so I was having a conversation with my friend and partner-in-mischief, Nilu Manji, at the back of the class. Suddenly I heard my name, and I looked at Nilu quizzically. Why was our teacher starting from the bottom of the class?

Nilu looked just as confused as I did, but my teacher called my name again, and moments later, there I was standing in front of the class with the two individuals who had ranked first and second. I had no idea I was even capable of this.

I couldn't wait to get my hands on my report card—one with no red ink to be found. I imagined the expression on my mom's face when I showed it to her. I ran home as fast as my legs could carry me and thrust my report card with As and Bs into her hands and proclaimed, "Look, Mom. No red grades!" Before she could even process what I'd said, I announced, "I ranked third in the class!"

She was just as shocked as I was. But once the shock wore off, she looked up from the flimsy paper with the black letters and gave me a big hug and an even bigger smile. "I knew you could do it," she said and kept staring at my report card with that big smile stuck on her face.

That brought me a deep and immeasurable sense of satisfaction. I was proud of myself. I felt good about making my mom so happy. Something within me shifted—it wasn't just the good grades but the *experience* that taught me I could rank among the top in my class if I applied myself and made studying my priority. From that point on, I did exactly that, because all that mattered to me was being ranked first in class and winning debates and knowledge competitions.

My family was poor, but so was every family that we associated with, so I never felt like I lacked anything. My childhood was joyful, but as I grew up, I realized that we were living hand to mouth, and it became more and more painful to watch my parents struggle to make ends meet. Since I was getting good grades, I figured I could get admission into a college (my new definition of success), and getting a college degree would lift my family out of poverty (my *why*).

It's important to point out that this was a very lofty definition of success: No one in my family had a college degree, and Mwanza had no education past tenth grade. And we had no money to pay for my college education.

I eventually graduated first in my tenth-grade class and left home at the age of 15 to live with my maternal uncle to complete high school in Dar es Salaam, Tanzania's capital city.

At age 18, I left the continent of Africa and attended Wadia College in Pune, India—three flights and a train ride away from home. Making this a reality was a struggle for my family. We couldn't qualify for a bank loan and searched hard to find anyone willing to lend us money for my flight and first year of college (today's equivalent of $500). Eventually, my mom received a loan from a woman whom everyone in town fondly referred to as Khursa Masi. Khursa Masi was not wealthy and had never gone to college herself, but she had a generous heart and a strong belief in educating young women.

During my first few weeks in India, I cried myself to sleep. I was hungry, lonely, and scared. Everyone there spoke English, and though I could read and write in English, I couldn't speak it well. The cafeteria served the same watery dal every day, along with tasteless vegetable curries that left me desperately homesick for my mom's flavor-packed food. I had grown up watching Indian movies where a woman who walked by herself would inevitably be pounced on, so I didn't feel safe walking outside the campus. Most of all, I missed my family very much, and I couldn't even hear their voices because they didn't own a phone. My parents didn't speak, read, or write English, so I learned to write letters in Gujarati, which, although it's my mother tongue, I'd never learned to read or write. I'd send off letters to them and wait anxiously for their reply.

Out of loneliness and misery, I thought about giving up—quitting college and flying back home. My negative mental chatter boomed: "Why am I putting myself through this torture? I don't even know if I'll be able to afford three years of college expenses, so why not cut my losses now? Women in Mwanza don't get college degrees. No one else in my family has a college degree, and they all have happy lives. Just go back."

I was on the verge of doing just that and flying back to Tanzania when a whole new set of thoughts entered into the debate. "Remember," I said to myself, "I wanted to lift my family out of poverty? I've got a real shot at doing that. I worked so hard to get here, and now I'm going to give up? I'll figure out a way to pay for the entire degree. Remember how grateful I was to have this chance of getting a college degree? I won't let my challenges take that away from me."

Luckily, the second set of thoughts was amplified, drowning out the first set. The moment I changed my thoughts and shifted them to focus on my definition of success, I saw the situation differently even though nothing had changed. I woke up with gratitude for the opportunity and had a spring in my step as I went to class. Without realizing it, I was exercising what I now refer to as my *Power Quotient*, or *PQ*. Your PQ is your ability to scan your mental chatter and intentionally choose an empowering response to a disempowering stimulus.

An empowering response is one that moves you closer to your definition of success. (I'll refer to PQ throughout the book and will share with you in Chapter 4 how and when I coined this term.)

INSIGHT

Embrace your power by intentionally choosing your response.

Because I was guided by the clear belief that a college degree would lift my family out of poverty, I overcame every challenge. Conversations about watery dal resulted in dinner invitations and sealed friendships with my lifelong friends Jehangir Dorabjee and Rukshi Mitha. I started enjoying my college experience. I paid for the rest of my college expenses by buying clothes from India and selling them in Tanzania. I graduated first class (the Indian equivalent of the dean's list) with a degree in mathematics, and more importantly, a recognition of my own resilience and resourcefulness.

What a nicely packaged success story, right? I got my mathematics degree, and we all lived happily ever after. Just kidding. If you don't know by now, let me be the first to tell you: Journeys to success are never that linear. Even though I had defined success with clarity and conviction, I hadn't actually looked deeply into whether achieving a degree would achieve my *why*.

Like many kids from poor families, I assumed a college degree was a one-way ticket to financial stability. But when I graduated from college and started looking for a job, I couldn't find anything that paid enough to lift us out of poverty—in fact, I wouldn't earn much more than if I didn't go to college.

I felt like a failure. I came close to giving up on my dream and settling for a job that neither excited me nor paid well. Every ounce of my being rebelled against this choice. Once again, I cried myself to sleep at night. My desire to get my family out of poverty haunted me.

Looking back, I celebrate this as a critical lesson in defining success. It isn't enough to come up with a checklist of achievements; you need to know that those achievements will actually serve your *why*. However, my struggles in India—the loneliness, the lack of tuition money, the fear of walking alone—made me more resilient and resourceful and gave me the confidence to enter uncharted territory, which in hindsight was success, but a different type of success.

While my definition of success hadn't changed, I knew I needed a new plan in order to achieve my *why*. In the midst of my postgraduation misery, I came upon a magazine called *PC World*. Two articles gripped me, one announcing that IBM had released its first personal computer and another about computer programming jobs in the United States. It was 1981, and personal computers were in their infancy. The tech sector was on the rise, and the jobs paid extremely well. The second article—about programming jobs—mentioned that people who were good at mathematics could easily translate those skills to program computers. I knew nothing about computers—I'd never even seen one, let alone used one—but if a degree in computer science was the path out of poverty for my family and me, that sounded great.

Applying for a computer science degree in North America was a struggle, but with the help of a family friend who was studying there, I applied to the University of Wisconsin in La Crosse. I was admitted, *and* I got a student visa. I was ecstatic!

> **INSIGHT**
>
> We don't always know it at the time, but what we consider failures are simply the foundations of future success.

My parents spent all their savings and I spent all my earnings to put together a total of $2,000. With nothing but that and a suitcase, I headed to Wisconsin in January 1983.

Take a second to imagine that: a girl who'd only ever lived in Tanzania and India, both tropical climates, going to Wisconsin for the first time in the winter. Luckily the International Students Association was used to this problem and met me at the airport with a spare coat and gloves!

Computer science degrees aren't easy for anyone, but I was on a particularly steep learning curve, since I'd never seen a computer in my life and I'd arrived 10 days after the semester had begun. On top of that, I had difficulty understanding American accents. Two weeks later, when I took my first quiz in my first computer science class, I earned a D for the first time since third grade. I wondered if I was capable of getting a degree in computer science. I broke down and sobbed. But I mustered the courage to ask for help. My very kind instructor, Keith Burand, stayed after hours to help me for many days. Honoring him when I received a distinguished alumni award from my alma mater in 2017 brought tears to his eyes and mine. Even though he had retired from teaching, he came to the event.

As a foreign student with limited work options, I was thrilled to learn I could work on campus. I worked 35 to 40 hours a week at the computer science center changing and stapling computer printouts. It was my first paying job. I was so happy and grateful to have this job that I poured my heart into it. The students as well as the staff noticed my attitude and my work. I'd get called in when someone didn't show up—which happened a lot during snowstorms; I was happy to walk in knee-deep snow to make my $3.30 an hour. I worked every Friday evening and on weekends as well as holidays. This, combined with a scholarship from the state of Wisconsin to pay in-state tuition and two summers of working full-time, took care of all my college expenses.

Ultimately, I graduated on the dean's list, with one big step to go: getting a job.

With only a one-year work visa, I had an exceptionally difficult time finding a job. Most companies wouldn't even consider interviewing me because of my visa status. But I kept trying, and I finally landed a job as a software developer at ETA Systems, a Minnesota-based startup that was building the world's fastest supercomputer. My yearly salary of $27,000 was more than my parents could earn in 10 years! My wildest dreams had come true. I'd achieved my vision of success and my *why*.

I struggled a lot when I started my career as you will read in Chapter 4. I felt very lucky to have a job and poured my heart into my work, but 3½ years later, ETA Systems shut down, and I was out of work.

Three months after losing my job, I joined IBM as a software developer in Rochester, Minnesota. Nine months later, for personal reasons, I wanted to move back to Minneapolis, but the only technical job available was that of a systems engineer, so I took it. Once again, I poured my heart into this job, which was much more aligned with my strengths. At the end of my first year in this position, I was named IBM's Rookie Systems Engineer of the Year and was sent on that luxe trip to San Francisco that I described earlier. I ranked at the top of more than 50 systems engineers that had joined IBM.

You can now understand how I was feeling as I walked down the hallway with Susan Whitney to the office of my manager's manager. In a matter of moments, I went from wondering if I belonged in that room of achievers (hello, impostor syndrome!) to realizing how hard I had worked to get there. I became grateful for the opportunities and my journey so far. And, most important, I realized that I had the potential to do more, to be more.

I work with so many women who also deal with impostor syndrome.

Whenever you feel that way, remember, it's all in your mind and you can shift your mindset. Understand that no one else can determine whether you belong somewhere or not—only you own that decision. Every time you wonder if you belong somewhere, tell yourself, "Yes I do! I worked hard to get here, and I've got the potential for even more success."

When Susan said to me, "You've got so much potential," one word struck something deep in me: "potential." She and my mother both knew I could do more; I could *be* more. My conversation with Susan had the same sparking effect as my mom's tears. They were both signals to me that there was more in me than I could see and I was inadvertently settling for less. The difference between now and then was that back then I knew exactly what I needed to do to get good grades.

But what did "potential" mean now? What was "success" to me now? I looked around at what others were doing. I wanted someone to emulate, someone to follow. But there was no one who looked like me, no one who I could relate to.

Susan's conversation kicked off a different level of thinking for me. I started *introspecting*—thinking about success, what it was and what it meant for me in my career and my life. Where did I want to be in five years? What did I want to do next and next after that? I began searching within, but I couldn't come up with an answer.

> **INSIGHT**
>
> When you know you've got potential, you'll dream bigger and be willing to take a chance on yourself.

Three months later, I became pregnant with my first child. Suddenly I started dreaming of a house with more space and a backyard with a swing, where my child could play. No one in my family or my husband's family had ever owned a house before, but now that I knew I had potential, it was as if I had given myself permission to dream bigger: I wanted to buy a house. That became my definition of success, and my *why* was for my daughter to swing in the backyard.

My salary, which had once seemed generous, was not enough to pay a home mortgage, so I started looking for opportunities that would increase my income. I discovered that a move into sales would allow me to earn more income, so I joined the sales team at IBM. Even though I knew nothing about sales, believing that I had potential, I took a chance on myself. I was stubbornly determined and motivated to succeed in this role. This decision pushed me completely outside my comfort zone. It pushed me to the edge of my competence and forced me to learn many new skills, as you will read in Chapter 3.

In six months, I began recognizing that I could learn and master new skills, and this gave me confidence in my ability to succeed in this role. We moved into our first home three weeks before my daughter, Sophia, was born.

Owning a home with a backyard swing set was another dream come true. And we even installed a baby swing. Every time I walked into my home, I was filled with gratitude. I put Sophia in her baby swing as soon as it was possible, and she loved it. Watching her smile from ear to ear in her swing made me even more grateful to have a job that made this possible.

At work, I was contributing value at my maximum capacity while experiencing tremendous growth, which created the perfect platform for me to excel. I was loving my work and my life! I could see and feel my own worth.

Within two years, I was ranked as one of the top salespeople on our team. This overwhelming feeling of success inspired me to aim higher and define my long-term definition of success: become a sales leader in five years. For the first time I had a clear understanding of where I wanted to be in five years. My *why* was to continue to provide well for my family, as I was pregnant with my second child and was continuing to help my parents.

My new long-term definition of success became my guiding light in every decision I made, and I set short-term (12-month) definitions to make sure I stayed on track to get there. They became stepping-stones to my long-term (5-year) vision. Whenever I faced a challenge—and there were many along my journey as you will read in the chapters that follow—I knew deep down where I was headed, and

INSIGHT

When you're stubbornly determined to achieve your success, nothing can stop you.

that gave me the staying power to learn from each challenge and keep moving forward with even more strength and resolve.

You'll come to learn as you keep reading that my definitions of success changed throughout my career as my life transformed, for both good and bad, and your definitions should, too.

Whenever I achieved one long-term vision of success, I created a new one and aimed even higher. Each achievement opened up new possibilities and gave me new insights that have formed the eight strategies of this book.

A STORY OF
INTENTIONAL SUCCESS

Vernā Myers
Vice President, Inclusion Strategy at Netflix

Vernā Myers's story is a great illustration of what can happen when you don't intentionally define success and how you can course-correct.

Upon graduating with a law degree from Harvard, I accepted a position in a prestigious law firm—mostly because it would help me pay off my student loans, the position coming with a hefty paycheck. Externally, it seemed like I'd found the perfect job in the perfect firm. Internally, I was frustrated by my day-to-day activities. The work didn't feel meaningful. The long hours made it impossible for me to do things outside of work that truly mattered to me. I especially didn't like the lack of lawyers of color in the firm.

After a few years, I read Mary Catherine Bateson's book *Composing a Life* and realized that I'm the only one who's the expert on my life. I don't have to do it like anyone else. I have the right to compose my own life.

This moment was scary—I wanted to make my parents proud, I worried about money, and more than anything else, I was questioning my identity. Who am I going to be if I'm not a lawyer? Will what I do next make me proud of myself? I knew I'd made all the right choices, I'd done all the work, and I'd played by the rules, but I was still unhappy! So I decided to make some changes. I know some people get into jams they can't get out of, but this wasn't a jam. This was just me making a choice.

So I made a new choice. I left my job. I relished my time with my four-year-old son, and talked to lots of people about where I was and where I wanted to go. I discovered that relationship building was a major strength of mine, which led me to become the executive director of a consortium of law firms that were focused on increasing racial diversity and building a community of lawyers of color in Boston firms. I loved this job and made some major connections in this role.

As I worked with lawyers from different walks of life and saw how much the deck was stacked against those from underrepresented groups, I realized diversity and inclusion (D&I) were my deepest values. So I started my own consulting firm, focused on D&I. My connections from my prior role became my clients.

After 20 years of consulting, one of those clients became Netflix. Soon enough, Netflix gave me a generous offer, complete with the flexibility I never had in previous full-time roles and agreed that I could keep my own company. It was an opportunity to test what I knew: After years of consulting for D&I programs, it was my turn to implement one. And the platform was tremendous. I could change tech and entertainment at the same time, as well as the stories being told.

Today, as the chief inclusion officer at Netflix, I've moved the needle significantly, and I'm a respected leading authority on D&I. None of it would have happened if I had settled for the traditional definition of success—wealth and prestige—and stayed in my first job. Now I spend my days helping to make Netflix a more diverse, welcoming, and safe place for employees of all kinds. And my compensation is higher than it's ever been.

INTENTIONAL EXERCISES

In each chapter, the Intentional Exercises section begins with Introspection, so you can gain self-knowledge and an understanding of where you currently stand with each intentional strategy. Next, we move to Application, where you'll apply the lessons from the chapter to accelerate your movement toward your success. Finally, we wrap up with Reflection and Celebration by reflecting on your past week, learning from it, course-correcting as needed, and celebrating your successes—both big and small—until you master your strategy.

The exercises in each chapter will help you to create and execute your strategy for success. I recommend that you take the time to do each exercise and apply what you've learned, to reap the benefits of the knowledge you've acquired in each chapter. This work will require deep thinking and searching. This is hard but necessary work. The results will be well worth the time and energy you put into it. Having said all that, if at any point you feel overwhelmed, take a break and come back.

In this chapter, we'll start with some introspection. Then, we'll apply the knowledge you gained in this chapter to establish your short- and long-term definitions of success. And we'll wrap up by ensuring you take time to reflect and celebrate your successes. Let's get started!

Introspection

Intentionally defining success is highly dependent on your understanding of yourself. The better you know who you are and what you want, the more precisely you'll be able to define success on your own terms. This self-knowledge will make you unstoppable and unshakable as you inevitably face challenges and naysayers. You'll be driven by your own internal compass and not external influences. Intentional introspection is a valuable career practice for gaining deeper self-knowledge. Are you ready to do the work? Good!

Answer the following questions as broadly or in as much detail as you like:

Understanding Yourself

- What are my core values? (These are nonnegotiable principles that are most important to you.)
- What energizes me or brings me joy?
- What are my strengths, and what do I excel at?
- What depletes me of my energy?
- What are my weaknesses? Or what don't I enjoy doing?
- What do I need to be financially self-sufficient?
- What motivates me to go to work every day?
- What about my work do I enjoy?
- What about my work do I wish were different?

Learning from Past Experiences

- When was the first time I saw potential in myself? How did I feel?
- What's the most recent achievement I'm proud of?
- What did I learn about myself in the pursuit of these achievements?
- What's important for me to thrive in a workplace? In the various places where I've worked, studied, or volunteered, what are some of the elements that enabled me to thrive?
- In thinking back to my favorite leader, what were that leader's qualities that empowered me and brought out the best in me?
- What team have I most enjoyed being part of, and what were the most important qualities of that team?
- What kind of a leader do I want to be? Whom do I want to lead? What kind of business do I want to lead?

Congratulate yourself for taking the time to answer these questions. This self-knowledge is key to your continued success. Intentionally defining your personal success and making sure your *why* is full of clarity and conviction are powerful sources of internal strength.

Introspection isn't a once-and-done exercise. As you learn more about yourself and as you change, come back to this exercise.

Application

Now that you've gained self-knowledge, let's create your personalized definitions of short- and long-term success.

Create Your Long-Term Definition of Success

Your vision of long-term success must include what's most important to you. It must be aligned with your core values, so it is deeply personal and meaningful. You must aim high to unlock the potential you know you have and be the reason you are excited to show up to work every day.

Your definition must also include both professional goals such as "Get promoted to a leadership role" and personal goals such as "Own a home for my child to grow up in." This will ensure you're successful inside and have a rich, fulfilling, and rewarding career and life.

As you'll read in the chapters that follow, at various points in my life, having a work-life balance, prioritizing my personal well-being, and taking care of my parents

INSIGHT

Externally visible success will ring hollow unless you feel successful within.

and children have all been part of my definition of success regardless of what my long-term career goal was at the time.

For me, if I hadn't been able to take care of my own well-being, my parents, and my children, no amount of externally visible success would've made me feel successful.

This is your time to think big and become all you're capable of becoming. Aim high, take a chance on yourself. Challenge the status quo.

You must know deep down that you've got tremendous potential—and you've no idea just how much. The only way to discover how much is to aim high and push yourself. You'll never know your capabilities until you test them. It's better to have tried and figured out what your limitations are than to settle for less than what you're capable of.

I've spoken to, mentored, and coached so many amazing women in the same position that I was in: terrific at their current jobs, but not planning an amazing future by aiming high.

As you read in my story, I was content with small successes by setting low expectations. I was achieving that success without pushing myself and without much effort. I was essentially shortchanging my potential. I was settling for less than what I was capable of.

You won't do that. Instead, you'll create a lofty vision that requires tremendous effort to achieve. And when you've got a lofty vision of the future, you'll strive to be your best every day and meet the daily challenges that come your way, because you'll know you're moving toward a greater vision.

To get started with this process, it's important to be in the right mindset. You should feel inspired, feel the tremendous potential in every ounce of your being, and feel the fire in your belly burning hot so you can aim high and create a lofty vision by shooting for the stars. I hope this chapter has you inspired, but if you're not there right now and you need to read your favorite inspirational quote (look back at Mae Jemison's at the start of the chapter if you'd like), or listen to a song, or read a poem that inspires you, or talk to someone who inspires you to dream big, go ahead and take a few minutes to do that. And then come back to this exercise while the content of this chapter is still fresh in your mind.

From this place of being fully inspired and knowing you've got tremendous potential, you're ready to define your long-term success. Start by answering the following questions:

- Five years from now, what would excite me and make me *feel* extremely successful? Your answer should make you want to jump up and down to tell your loved ones what you've achieved. Something that will make you say to yourself: "That was hard! Wow! I did it!"
- Why does this vision make me so excited?
- Five years from now, who would I be proud to be?
- Why is this version of me so inspiring?

Pay special attention to the *why*, because that's what will drive your behavior not just to pursue your success but especially to persevere when the pursuit gets challenging—which it should if you've aimed high.

Because you're reading this book, I assume that getting a leadership position is in your long-term definitions of success. At a minimum, getting promoted must be. Depending on your role, you might have many levels of promotions before you're considered for a leadership role.

Through the mere act of knowing you have leadership potential and aiming high, you are developing a leadership mindset and embarking upon a leadership journey.

Understand that a leadership mindset is one where you see potential in yourself and others. It's also a mindset where you learn from your past, but that doesn't allow your past to encumber you; it's a mindset that accepts and is appreciative of where you currently are and who you are—*and* knows you can be more and do more.

Leadership starts in your mind and then manifests in your behavior. You behave like a leader the day you start taking the necessary steps to realize your leadership potential. That behavior will eventually earn you a role and a title that comes with the responsibility of leading people in your organization. We'll dive deeper into leadership behavior in the remaining chapters.

Start brainstorming your definition now. Remember to include both personal and professional goals. Have as many as five goals.

If you need some help getting started, let me share some examples of my goals from various stages in my life. Remember, I'm sharing these just to give you ideas. You must come up with your own definition of success.

- I will lift my family out of poverty.
- I will emerge as a respected leader who inspires others to follow.
- I will become an IBM executive.
- I will support my parents financially.
- I will join boards of organizations that cultivate young women leaders.

- I will make time to mentor other women and underrepresented minorities.
- I will start a scholarship at my alma mater for women of color.
- I will build a secondary school in rural Tanzania to provide access to higher education.
- I will help deserving young women in Tanzania obtain a college education.
- I will write a book to help women emerge as leaders and become changemakers to create gender parity in leadership roles.

Once you've got your definition of long-term success, a good test for whether you're on the right track is to answer some simple questions for each one individually:

- Am I energized to pursue this with everything I've got?
- Do my *whys* matter so much that no matter what comes my way, they'll keep me going?
- Is my definition clear?
- Is this something I *want* to do versus something I *should* do?
- Is it deeply personal and meaningful?
- Is it aligned with my core values?
- Am I aiming high and stretching myself personally and professionally?
- Does it scare me?
- Will it grow my impact and influence?
- Does it force me outside my comfort zone?

If your answer to any of these questions is no, go back to your long-term definition of success and refine it. Keep working on it until you say yes to each question. Once you've done that, congratulate yourself because you now have a long-term definition of success!

The good news is that this is *your* definition, and you can change it any time you want! As you embark upon your journey to your success, more possibilities will open up, Your definition of success will, and should, change based on where you are in your life and in your career. As you change and grow, as your circumstances change, your definition should also change. The purpose of intentionality is never to keep you trapped; instead, it's to ensure you move forward with purpose.

Your vision of success makes sure you're consciously aware of where you're going, so that you'll always be advancing toward it. When you connect to your personal definition of success with clarity and conviction, it will guide you like a laser beam to your target. It will become your primary factor in every decision, your lifeline in every conundrum, and your barometer for every set of thoughts. You can prioritize what's actually important, because no matter what's happening, you're still clear about what you want and where you're going. It becomes a built-in filter for distractions that don't move you closer to your definition of success. And in the event you get off track, you'll be able to dust yourself off and keep moving forward stronger.

Create Your Short-Term Definition of Success

Now that you know where you want to be in five years and who you want to become, you're ready to create your short-term definition of success, which is a stepping-stone toward making your long-term definition of success a reality.

Let's assume that in your long-term definition of success, one of your professional goals is to emerge as a leader, and your short-term definition of success has a professional goal to excel in your current role and get rated one of the highest on your team.

First and foremost, you must make sure you're in a role that's a good fit for you. What does that role look like exactly? It should have the potential for you to do the following:

- Maintain a healthy work-life balance (Chapter 3).
- Contribute value at your maximum capacity (Chapter 4).
- Grow your competence and confidence (Chapter 5).
- Build relevant and meaningful relationships (Chapter 6).
- Build a leadership brand (Chapter 7).
- Have upward mobility (Chapter 8).

If your current position isn't the right fit, you must make it a priority to find a position that is. Only then will you be able to excel at your role and get rated one of the highest on your team. I say that your role must have the "potential" for the above qualities because you won't actually know until you try it.

Your career is a long-term game. Feel free to explore different options that seem interesting until you find the right fit. You don't know what you don't know, so be open to exploring and learning. The important thing is to never settle in a role that isn't the right fit—instead, explore other options.

I moved from software development to systems engineering to sales, which was my perfect fit. But whatever role you're in—even if it's not a great fit—perform it at the best of your capability and intentionally use it as a "learning and growing platform" until you move into a position that's a better fit. Learn more about yourself and the environment you thrive in—in terms of the culture of your organization as well as that of your boss and teammates; this will help you make better choices in the future.

To get started on crafting your short-term definition of success, answer the following question:

- What do I need to achieve personally and professionally in the next 12 months so I can move closer to my long-term definition of success?

Unpack your definition and break it down into specific goals. Be sure to have no more than five goals.

Some examples of my short-term definitions of success over the course of my career are:

- Become one of the highest-performing individuals on my team.
- Build a meaningful relationship with my boss.
- Seek opportunities to engage senior executives.
- Lead a complex project for a tough client.
- Prioritize time with my children.
- Take my children on an annual vacation.
- Pay for my father's heart surgery.
- Find assignments that will force me outside my comfort zone.
- Build a respected leader's brand.
- Prioritize self-care.

Intentionally defining your short- and long-term definitions of success with clarity and conviction are powerful sources of internal strength you can tap into whenever needed.

As you read the rest of the chapters in this book, take what things resonate with you and add them to your short- and long-term definitions of success.

This exercise is meant to be one that you can (and should) come back to again and again. In fact, I encourage you to save every version to look back on whenever you need a dose of inspiration. Every year or whenever your life situation changes, revisit your definitions of success and make sure they still work for you—if not, change them! Remember, your definitions of success should change with you. Don't feel stuck with a goal that's no longer serving you.

Reflection and Celebration

In order to keep moving toward your success with enthusiasm and energy, it's important to set aside a weekly reflection time to look back, learn, course-correct and, most importantly, celebrate small successes. In the next chapter, we'll talk about scheduling a weekly reflection time.

Celebrating yourself and your efforts is key to getting and staying energized in the pursuit of achieving long-term success. Often women get so busy moving from success to success that they don't stop to reflect upon how far they've come and celebrate. They only see how far they have to go, which can get exhausting. Honor your hard work and cultivate a success mindset, because emerging as a leader is a long game.

> **INSIGHT**
>
> Internalize and honor your success to scale new heights.

Tell yourself you're proud of *you*. There's no hubris in knowing you worked hard and it paid off. Celebrating success also means when someone compliments you on a job well done, don't wave it away. Acknowledging your achievements isn't bragging; it's just recognizing the facts!

Reward yourself in a way that makes you feel special. The bigger and tougher the achievement, the bigger the reward. For weekly or monthly achievements, it can be a spa treatment. For bigger efforts that lead to bigger achievements that take years to attain, celebrate in a major way, like taking the entire family on a vacation, flying first class, or buying yourself something special. Whatever it is, make this reward something you wouldn't normally treat yourself to. The idea is to feel the gratitude of what success can make possible for you and your family.

Once you've truly soaked in the gratitude and success of your accomplishments, do the work to determine your next long-term definition of success. Keep aiming higher and rising up your career ladder until you make it up to the very top.

When I became a single mother, I decided that every year for my birthday I'd treat myself to a piece of jewelry I previously never could have imagined I could afford—because I worked really, really hard to balance my work and my life to achieve my vision of success. For my milestone birthdays, I went big on treating myself to more exquisite pieces. They still serve as a reminder of the times when I was so proud of myself for achieving what I did.

Today, expensive gifts for myself don't hold the same significance, so instead I celebrate quietly by thinking about the experience and being in a state of gratitude and awe. I also celebrate by donating to my favorite causes. The key is to really reward yourself with what makes you feel special because you deserve to feel special. Feel the success in the very core of your being so you can internalize the importance of what you've achieved, and let it motivate you to reach even higher next time.

SET YOUR INTENTIONS

Promise yourself:

- I will create a deeply personal and meaningful lofty vision of success.
- I will pursue my success with everything I've got.
- I will build a success mindset by celebrating and internalizing my successes.

2

INTENTIONAL ATTENTION

Your actions express your priorities.
MAHATMA GANDHI

THE SECOND strategy that will help you show your worth and emerge as a leader is Intentional Attention, and in this chapter we'll focus on how you intentionally allocate your most valued, limited, and perishable asset: your attention for meaningful progress toward your vision of success.

It's important to understand why *attention* is our most important resource instead of *time*. In our era of multitasking, most of us have devices tied to us with a constant stream of emails, text messages, and other alerts. Being present in the moment is one of our major challenges. If you're not intentional, you might be in a meeting physically, but you aren't fully present mentally or emotionally. In those situations, you're giving the meeting and people there your time, but not your attention—and that's a very big distinction to make.

What differentiates your success from another person's depends on why and where you allocate your attention. Success is achieved on a daily basis by intentionally investing your attention for maximum returns.

Let me share my story of how I learned the importance of intentionally allocating my attention to achieve my vision of success.

Driven by my desire to buy a house in which to raise my daughter, I wanted to make more money, so I decided to join the sales team at IBM. That position pushed me completely outside my comfort zone. I felt like a fish out of water. In my prior jobs as a software developer and a systems engineer, my projects were well defined and handed to me, so it was easy for me to successfully complete those projects while working 40 to 45 hours a week. In this new role, I knew what business outcomes I had to achieve but had no idea how to achieve them.

My sales leader, Keith Elzia, ran our organization using a Success Plan that enabled him to achieve his quarterly and yearly business outcomes predictably and consistently. This plan had a list of his key deals he referred to as "must-wins." He structured his days around those deals and held review calls with each of us to ensure progress was being made on those deals.

I thought that was a brilliant way of running a business, so I decided to create my own Personal Success Plan (PSP) to achieve my business outcomes (aka my short-term definition of success). The only difference was the fact that he was an expert at running his business, and I was just starting out.

As a new sales representative, I was energetic, eager, and enthusiastic and was determined to succeed. I had a list of over 50 deals I could possibly work on. I made every single one of them my "must-wins" and added them to my PSP.

Each of these deals had multiple tasks associated with them, which created an endless list of tasks. Every day, I worked on as many tasks as I possibly could. Despite the fact that I was super-busy and putting in 60-hour workweeks, I wasn't actually making meaningful progress on any of my deals.

I was under the impression that the longer I worked, the more tasks I'd complete, and that would lead me to win some deals.

All day long, I was working hard moving from task to task but not making any meaningful progress. I was caught in a task trap that led me to wonder if this job was a fit for me at all.

> **INSIGHT**
>
> You've got limited time and energy. Invest them for maximum returns.

During my first review meeting with Keith, I ran through my endless task list of all my deals. I told him I was working long hours and was willing to work even more hours so I could win some deals. Once I was done sharing my extensive list, Keith said something to me that became a game changer for my success: "Working more hours isn't necessarily the answer; it's about priorities."

Then he explained: "Shelmina, when I first became a sales representative, I was just like you. Energetic, enthusiastic, and eager to succeed. I worked very long hours, chased every deal in my pipeline, and I didn't make much progress. I was extremely frustrated."

When I asked for his help to achieve my business outcomes, he opened my eyes to see that I was working on too many deals, which was in turn diluting my attention. I was giving each deal the same priority and performing tasks with no consideration of how it impacted my business outcomes.

Going forward, he recommended I pick a few deals that gave me the best chance of achieving my business outcomes.

I looked at him, confused.

He continued: "We all have limited time and energy. The key to achievement is to use your time and energy wisely. Only work on deals that will maximize your chances of success. There are not enough hours in the day for you to chase every deal in your pipeline—that's just the nature of our business. You must learn to qualify and prioritize your deals. Pick the deals that are worthy of your attention."

"Worthy of my attention?" I asked, baffled.

"Yes. You see, any attention you use working on a deal you can't win, you take away from one you can potentially win. You must qualify each deal to determine which deals are most worthy of your attention based on your chances of winning them. These are your 'must-win' deals."

With his coaching, everything started to make sense and turned my thinking upside down. I also felt rejuvenated and excited to make meaningful progress instead of being weighed down by my endless task list.

INSIGHT

Always be asking: "Is this worthy of my attention?"

I qualified each deal by determining the possibility and probability of winning it. First, I made sure it was possible for me to win that deal, and then I determined what the probability was. I created a list of my must-win deals, and this time the list included 15 instead of all 50. Winning these 15 deals would mean I'd exceed my sales targets by 20 percent. I added my must-win deals to my PSP.

Keith had such an incredible way of coaching me that I'll be forever grateful for. Learning that he had the same struggles and overcame them gave me the confidence that I would, too.

Going into the meeting, my concern was whether *I* was worthy of the role. I never considered whether the deals were worthy of me and *my* attention. Asking the simple question "Is this worthy of my attention?" changed my entire approach not just for my deals but for everything else in my life that vied for my attention.

SAY NO

The next lesson I had to learn is one so many women struggle with both in and out of the workplace: saying *no*. In this part of my life, I needed to learn to say no to deals that weren't my must-wins.

Saying no to the stakeholders whose deals I chose not to work on was hard for me. I was new to my role and wanted everyone to like me, and I thought that saying no to working on a deal would mean the stakeholders wouldn't like me. So I approached Keith again and asked for his guidance on how to say no without being disliked. (I also wanted to make sure he was on my side if a stakeholder complained to him after I said no to working on their deal.)

After I explained my situation to Keith, he said, "If you don't say no to the deals that don't deserve your attention, you won't be able to say yes to the deals that do."

> **INSIGHT**
>
> If you don't say no to what doesn't deserve your attention, you won't be able to say yes to what does.

He continued: "Remember, you're not hired to win a popularity contest. You're hired to deliver business outcomes. You must become comfortable saying no to what doesn't deserve your attention. It's not important that people like you. It's important that they respect you."

He went on to explain that when you deliver business outcomes, you'll earn respect.

How You Say No Makes All the Difference

For most women, saying no is difficult for multiple reasons. In addition to our desire to be liked, we want to be seen as collaborative and as a team player. We feel guilty saying no because we think it comes across as selfish or makes us seem difficult to work with. On the contrary, saying no to what is not aligned with your highest priorities is *necessary* to deliver the maximum business outcome not just for you but also for your boss. It's truly a win-win, and you must see it as such. Many women believe that saying no means they have to deliver bad news, but the reality is that it's not bad news when it benefits you and your organization.

On the other hand, you might think that saying yes will please people and they'll like you. The fact is, pleasing people doesn't mean you'll be liked. When you say yes to a project that will hinder your achievement, you'll eventually lose respect. Always be driven by doing what's right for yourself *and* for your organization, not pleasing individual people.

> **INSIGHT**
>
> Aspire to be respected—
> not to be liked.

Having said that, this two-letter word can be met with a lot of resistance, causing unnecessary friction, added tension, and strained relationships if not done with care. How you say no makes all the difference. Your style, your attitude, and your choice of words matter.

Depending on what you're saying no to and to whom you're saying it, it might be as easy as "I'm currently committed to other priorities and can't take on this project."

However, when you're dealing with a politically charged situation or you've got powerful stakeholders, the conversation becomes more complicated.

Let me take you through three steps to have this conversation in a productive manner in order to maximize the business outcomes for everyone involved.

Step 1. Prepare for the Conversation

Prepare for the conversation by writing down your point of view so you can effectively explain why you're saying no. Keep the following in mind as you prepare:

- Stay focused on maximizing business outcomes for your organization. (Remember, when you're talking to people whose project or deal you're not going to work on, the focus has to be on the fact that you're prioritizing what's best for the overall organization.)
- Explain that you've weighed their requests against your other commitments and business priorities. Focus on why the decision is right for you *and* the overall business. Don't make it about them. You're not saying no to them; you're saying no to the task/project.
- Choose appropriate words that show this is a sound business decision versus an excuse. Use sentences like "I'm prioritizing my time to maximize business outcomes. My current priorities and commitments are (insert them here)."
- Don't use statements that make you sound like a victim or are personal such as "I wish I had more time to work on your project." Remember that it's not about time; it's about priorities.

Step 2. Set Your Intentions Before the Conversation

Before you have the conversation, set the following intentions:

- Doing the right thing for the overall business
- Being sincere and transparent
- Being kind and firm
- Gaining their respect
- Listening to their perspectives
- Changing your decision if necessary
- Strengthening your relationship

Determining how you want to have this conversation before you sit down together will drive your behavior during the conversation. Remember that pleasing people and being kind aren't the same thing. You should always be kind, no matter what.

Step 3. Have the Conversation

Start the conversation by making it clear that you'd like to share your point of view and also get theirs.

Next, share your point of view in accordance with the intentions you've set, and explain why you're saying no in a clear, concise, and convincing way.

After you've shared your thoughts, the next step is critical. You must ask the others for their perspective. You can do this by asking a question like "What are your thoughts?" Be sure never to use self-doubting questions like "Does my perspective make sense?"

Give them time to formulate a response, and truly be open and seek to understand their perspective with your undivided attention.

If they share something that you didn't consider, acknowledge it with statements like "I hadn't thought of that," "That's a really good point," or "Thank you for making me aware."

By keeping an open mind and respecting their opinions, you'll deepen relationships regardless of the outcome of the conversation.

If you learn something you didn't know that makes you reconsider your decision, do that. Don't be afraid to change your decision. And don't be afraid to admit you're wrong. Don't get your ego tied up in your decision. Always be open to changing your decision if a new one makes more sense. And be sure not to get defensive, since that indicates a lack of confidence in your decision.

After you hear people out, if you still believe your decision is the right decision, you must own it. Stand your ground in a kind and firm manner. Let them know that you appreciate their perspective, and state that you believe sticking to your current priorities and commitments is the right thing to do in order to maximize the organization's business outcomes. Should something change, let them know you'll be back in touch with them.

The first few times you have a conversation like this, you'll most likely be uncomfortable. That's normal and expected. The more you practice saying no and standing up for what's the right thing for you and your organization, the better you'll get at it. Saying no doesn't come naturally, but it's a skill you can and must learn.

Keep in mind that there will always be some people who don't like you or the decisions you make, and that's OK; you can't control them. Don't let them bother you. As long as you know deep down that you're doing the right thing for yourself and for your organization, that's all that matters.

STRUCTURE YOUR DAYS AROUND YOUR PRIORITIES

When you say no to what's not worthy of your time and attention, you're saying yes to what's worthy—your priorities. In order to maximize your achievement, you must focus your attention on your highest priorities by structuring your days around them.

After the conversation I had with Keith, recounted earlier in this chapter, I became very intentional about focusing all my attention and energy on my must-win deals. They took priority over everything else. For every deal I chose to pursue, I created a list of tasks, meetings, and activities required to make progress on the deal and scheduled them on my calendar.

> **INSIGHT**
>
> When you intentionally focus your attention on your highest priorities, you move from being busy to productive.

Every business day was structured around my priorities instead of my endless task list. As soon as I did this, I was no longer busy—I was productive. I started making meaningful progress on my must-win deals every hour of every business day. I achieved a lot more in a shorter period of time.

And whenever a new deal came up, I was able to quickly determine if that deal should take priority over my current must-win deals in my PSP based on whether or not it would improve my chances of success.

Schedule Time to Recharge

When I started structuring my entire day around my priorities, I realized that I wasn't able to bring my best-quality attention to all my tasks when they were scheduled back-to-back. Because of this, I scheduled five minutes after every task to decompress from the last task and get energized and ready for the next one. During that break, I often got up from my desk, took a walk, and focused on my breathing. This not only centered me, but also allowed me to compartmentalize, be completely present with my tasks, and increase my productivity. Find the ideal amount of time and activities that do the same for you.

> **INSIGHT**
>
> Pause and recharge to gather energy for increased productivity.

Schedule Time for Other Tasks

Initially, I started scheduling my entire day around my priorities and realized that there were other tasks and business needs that were falling through the cracks and needed my attention. I quickly learned that I needed to schedule time for those tasks as well. I asked myself this question every time a task was put on my plate: "How much of my attention does this task deserve, and when does it deserve it?" The answer to that question became crucial when scheduling my days.

For example, I received many emails throughout the day. Instead of constantly responding to them, I decided how much and when I'd allocate my attention to emails and scheduled it on my calendar. I found that 15 minutes first thing in the morning, 15 minutes every 2 hours, and 15 minutes at the end of the day for emails was the perfect formula for me. I also prioritized my emails and responded to all the urgent and important emails first and then handled the less important and nonurgent ones. If I ever felt like I was falling behind, I'd allocate an additional 30 minutes the following week.

I also scheduled 30 minutes for my "administrative tasks" once every week at the end of a day.

Through trial and error, I found out that scheduling 80 percent of my calendar for my highest priorities left enough time for me to complete the other tasks I needed to handle.

This new way of scheduling my day meant I was intentionally allocating time to everything on my calendar! Each task got my undivided attention. Nothing important ever fell through the cracks, and nothing insignificant wasted my precious attention.

In the Intentional Exercises section of this chapter, I'll teach you how you can create, execute, and master the strategy of Intentional Attention.

BEST USE OF YOUR ATTENTION

As I became more and more intentional about allocating my attention, I began to notice tasks that were consuming a lot of my attention and started asking if they were worthy of that. I asked myself, "Will this provide the best return in terms of achieving my business outcomes?" and "Could I have used my attention elsewhere?"

As I took inventory of what was consuming my attention, I came to realize that even though I set aside time for emails and phone calls, I was spending too much of it responding to questions about the status of my must-win deals. My stakeholders wanted to know how I was doing, partly because I was new in my role and hadn't proved myself and partly because they wanted to be informed of my progress. Many were offering to help, all with good intentions, but the number of emails and phone calls was getting out of hand and taking away precious attention I could be spending making progress on deals.

I talked to my stakeholders and came up with a win-win so they could get what they wanted and I could get what I wanted. They wanted to be kept informed of the status of my deals, and I wanted to spend less time responding to their individual requests and more time making progress on the deals. We jointly agreed that I'd send out status reports every Friday that would include updates on every deal. If I needed any help, I'd reach out. I blocked Friday afternoons on my calendar and consistently sent out status reports. The emails and phone calls stopped. It freed up over an hour of my time every day.

> **INSIGHT**
>
> You teach others to respect your time when you respect your time yourself.

Intentionally allocating my attention was the beginning of my ability to move closer to my definition of success on a daily basis. My productivity was better than ever before, and it was reflected in the progress I was making on my deals. Within three months, I started winning some of those deals, too! This gave me the confidence to buy a house six months after I started my new role, which happened to be three weeks before my daughter, Sophia, was born!

My performance gained me respect. And the more deals I won, the easier it became for me to say no to deals that weren't my must-wins. Soon people accepted my no easily, as they trusted that my decisions were based on maximizing not just my business outcomes but also those of our organization.

In hindsight, moving into sales became one of my best career decisions, and learning to ask the question "Does this deserve my attention?" became one of the best lessons I learned in my career.

My strategy of Intentional Attention was instrumental in helping me achieve my business objectives (aka my short-term definition of success) at the end of the year. For the following year, I changed my short-term definition of success to getting one of the highest performance ratings. When I achieved that, for the first time I had a long-term definition of success: to become a sales leader in five years. I added that to the very top of my PSP. As I progressed in my career, I created and executed six other strategies that I'll share with you in the remainder of the chapters, and they all became priorities on my PSP.

My Personal Success Plan started out as a document with a list of my must-win deals that were my priorities so I could structure my day around them to make meaningful progress. It evolved into a full-fledged PSP that had my short- and long-term definitions of success, my goals that would enable me to achieve my success, and all my personal and professional priorities. I used my PSP during my weekly reflection time (we will talk about this later in this chapter) to make sure I never lost sight of what I decided mattered most. It not only laid the foundation for my ability to achieve all my future definitions of success, but also helped me achieve work-life balance, as you'll read in the next chapter.

A STORY OF INTENTIONAL ATTENTION

Johanna Maska
CEO of Global Situation Room, Inc.

Regardless of how well you structure your days around your priorities, in today's fast-paced, unpredictable, and uncertain environment, things don't always work as planned, and you must be prepared to reconsider your priorities "in the moment." When this happens, having clear priorities helps you make the right choice. This is illustrated brilliantly in the story my friend Johanna Maska shares with us when she served as White House Director of Press Advance for President Barack Obama.

My family had always been Midwestern conservatives. My father was not pleased when I registered as a Democrat.

When I watched Barack Obama speak at the Democratic National Convention in 2004, he spoke to everything I cared about: the changing economy in Illinois, his family's hardworking Kansas values, and the need for our country to find unity in moments of despair and move with purpose toward the world as it should be. I knew right then and there that I'd do anything to work for Barack Obama.

My journey to work for him was indirect. First I worked for a governor, then in a gubernatorial race, and then in state government. In the earliest days of the 2008 Obama presidential campaign, I got my chance to join the campaign, only after successfully making my case—with stellar references and freshly baked bread—to the state director.

From the beginning of the Iowa caucuses in 2007 until 2015, I worked as part of Barack Obama's advance teams. Every detail counted. Advance teams are often an old boys' club, but our campaign was trying to be different, and I was the first female member of the Iowa advance team—and joining it without having any family connections. While my role was engaging the press, my attention was always on the people in the audience. After all, their experience would determine their vote. In this role, I had the opportunity to set the stage for Barack and Michelle Obama to address every type of forum. A community college event in Iowa, a rally in Idaho, election night 2008.

It all happened so fast. In one moment, I went from working on a campaign to working for the president elect. In the next moment, I was helping to arrange an inaugural; and in the next, I was working for the president of the United States of America. An unlikely one. One without family connections. One whose first name differed from the customary George, Bill, John.

In the scheduling and advance department, we were in charge of President Obama's most important asset: his time. For the president, every hour of the day matters. There are conversations at every level of government, but the only ones that make it to a president's calendar are the things no one else can get done.

I was fortunate that President Obama was disciplined and predictable. We didn't need to worry about coming up with lists of places for him to eat and entertain himself. On trips, he inevitably wanted to go back to his room, have his broccoli and chicken, play some cards, and go to sleep.

Politics, on the other hand, is never predictable. We had a calendar for the entire year, broken out by week, broken out by day, and broken down to the meeting—and I still do this in my current role; this is how I operate. We had an idea when global summits would happen, when leaders' meetings would happen, when different things were on his schedule. Every day, we had an agenda of what we were trying to accomplish.

But every morning, we woke up to every headline and every story around the world, and frantic emails: "We need to respond to this!" "We need to do this!" It's said the Obama administration produced more emails in the first eight months than in the first eight years of the Bush administration. You can't just pay attention to what you've already planned; you need to pay attention to what's happening in the world.

There were days when I was already on the plane to a reelection campaign event, and then there was a massive event like a shooting in Colorado. And you can't go on with a campaign event when there's been a tragedy like that; you need to be sensitive to the changing dynamic. You need to be responsive. I'd literally be texting in a taxiing plane, trying to communicate with the press off the record on next steps before any public statements were issued.

To make quick, thoughtful decisions, you need to have discerning judgment and recognize that the game is always changing. You need to understand the severity of current events. And you need to be crystal clear on your priorities. My priority was always: "What would the American people want their president to do? Would they want the president to keep fighting for his job, or would they want the president to care about their lives?"

INTENTIONAL EXERCISES

Here, we'll use the definitions of success you created in Chapter 1 and start to create your strategy of Intentional Attention so you can move closer to your vision of success every day. As you start executing and mastering your strategy of Intentional Attention, you'll achieve more in every hour of every day than you ever did before.

We'll start with the Introspection section so you can gain knowledge of how you're currently allocating your attention; then we'll move to the Application section to apply the insights you learned to create and execute your strategy of "Intentional Attention" today, and we'll wrap things up with Reflection and Celebration to look back, course-correct, and celebrate your success of applying this strategy until you master it. Let's get started.

Introspection

First, let's focus on the following questions in order to understand how you currently use your most valued, limited, and perishable asset: your attention.

Ask yourself about the structure of your day:

- Are my business days structured around my highest priorities or around an endless list of tasks?
- On most days, do I feel like I am busy or productive?
- Am I productive throughout my working day?
- How do I prioritize my tasks?
- When I've got competing priorities, how do I pick?
- How do I decide what to say yes to and what to say no to?
- When do I best handle my most challenging tasks?

Now ask yourself about the best use of your attention:

- How much time do I spend on emails? Can I prioritize my emails better?
- Do I waste my precious attention complaining about situations outside my control (such as the weather, traffic, or a tool I hate but must use at work)?
- Do I let people or situations upset me and waste my precious attention?

- How much time do I spend on consuming information that's not aligned with moving closer to my success (for example, breaking news, social media, etc.)?
- How is my ability to compartmentalize my tasks and give my full undivided attention?

Next, look at every day on your calendar for the past two weeks and answer these questions:

- Did I allocate my attention to my highest priorities?
- What stopped me from allocating my attention to my highest priorities? Give five specific examples.
- Did I move closer to my definition of success?
- What stopped me from moving closer to my definition of success? Give five specific examples.
- When was I depleted of energy? How can I recharge and restore my energy levels?

Application

Now, let's create and execute your strategy of Intentional Attention with three steps:

1. Create your PSP.
2. Structure your days around your priorities.
3. Schedule other tasks.

Step 1. Create Your PSP

Create a new document called My Personal Success Plan. At the top, write your long-term definition of success, followed by your short-term definition of success from Chapter 1.

For the purpose of this exercise, let's assume your long-term definition of success includes to emerge as a leader and one aspect of your short-term definition of success includes achieve your business objectives.

Next, write down your business objectives for the year. Your business objectives are detailed descriptions of what your boss expects you to deliver. Most companies have a formal process in which an individual's personal business objectives are shared in writing. (Typically, at review time, you'll be evaluated on your business objectives.) If you don't have personal objectives against which your success will be measured, you must get your objectives in writing from your boss. A short and simple email like this will get you started: "It's my desire to deliver business outcomes that exceed your expectations. Please let me know your availability in the next two weeks so I can clearly understand your expectations of me."

Many women I work with get shortchanged on their evaluations because their business objectives either aren't clear or are subjective (for example, "Bring on six new clients" versus the subjective "Bring on some new clients"). It's impossible to achieve or exceed your objectives if you don't know exactly what they are and how you'll be measured against them.

Once you're clear on your objectives for the year, break them down into quarterly and monthly objectives so you can be sure you accomplish everything you need to by the end of the year. Once you've done that work, add these objectives to your PSP. These are your "must-achieve" objectives.

Determine Your Priorities

Next determine your priorities for each business objective.

To determine your priorities, look at each objective individually and ask the question, "What's the one thing I can do to maximize my chances of achieving this business objective?" The answer to that question is now your first priority.

Once you've got your topmost priority, keep asking this question to create a list of your highest priorities. Be sure to not dilute your focus by having too many priorities, so work to keep this list to a maximum of 10.

As you start mastering this strategy, you'll know how many priorities are needed to achieve each of your business objectives and, just as important, how many priorities you can handle at one time.

Once your list of priorities is finalized, share it with your boss, your mentors, and others whom you trust and admire. Getting their feedback will ensure you're focusing your attention on the priorities that will maximize your chances of achieving your business outcomes and make your short-term definition of success a reality. If necessary, refine your priorities based on their responses.

Add your priorities to your PSP. As you read the remainder of the chapters, you'll add more priorities to your PSP. Each of these priorities will accelerate your journey toward achieving your definition of success.

Step 2. Structure Your Days Around Your Priorities

Now that your priorities are clear, it's time to schedule them to ensure they get done. What does not get scheduled may not get your attention, so it's critical to schedule and structure your days around your priorities. Go ahead and unpack each of your priorities from Step 1 into actionable tasks that can be scheduled.

Next, determine when those tasks should be scheduled to provide the best chance of success. Pay special attention to scheduling the most challenging task at the most opportune time for you—in terms of both what day of the week and what time of the day work best. Personally, I schedule my most challenging tasks early in the day at the start of the week, as that's when I'm at my absolute best. This also starts my day and week off with a big win, because I completed a hard task early, giving me momentum to keep executing my other tasks. You should experiment to determine when you're personally able to handle different kinds of tasks best.

Recognize that we're humans and not machines. People don't operate at the same capacity all the time. There are times when you operate at your highest levels (when you can get lots done with accuracy in a short period of time), and there are times when you operate at a slightly lower level. An understanding of how you operate best puts you in a position of power when it comes to scheduling your most difficult and challenging tasks.

Keep in mind that your priorities shouldn't take up more than 80 percent of your calendar, because you need to save 20 percent of your attention for the other tasks, which we'll discuss in Step 3.

Select your tasks/meetings/activities associated with your highest priorities, and add them to your calendar as early as possible. Look at what you currently have, and determine if it should be there or not. Say no to anything that's not a priority. Ask your boss to help you prioritize if needed.

Schedule time for breaks to recharge so you'll be at your maximum productivity level for every task through the day.

As soon as your days are structured around your priorities and you're able to give your undivided best-quality attention to every task, you'll experience productivity levels you've never known before. You'll start making meaningful progress every day and move closer to your vision of success. You'll be astounded by how much you're able to achieve in a short time frame.

If your calendar is more than 80 percent full, you have too many priorities and will need to rank them. Seek help from your boss if necessary, especially if you're new in your role, but keep in mind that the ultimate ownership of your priorities rests with you.

Also be aware that there will be times when what's important is dictated by something that's not a priority for you right now but matters a great deal in the long run. A high-priority task from your boss should fall in this category, and even though it may not count toward your personal business outcomes, that task should be made into your priority and scheduled accordingly. Remember, your boss's priority is your priority.

Be cautious here though. Some women I've worked with had bosses continually send them work that didn't contribute toward what they eventually would be rated on. If this becomes a rule instead of an exception, explain your situation to your boss and make your boss a partner in prioritizing your tasks. Remember, your business achievement counts toward your boss's business achievement, so it's in your boss's best interest that you're maximizing your achievement.

Your achievements will speak for themselves, and you'll earn people's respect. Also, as people start to realize that you only allocate your attention to priorities that deliver maximum business outcomes, they'll stop coming to you with lesser priorities. Slowly but surely, anything that's not worth your valuable attention will be weeded out as a result.

Your PSP will also become your lifeline when your environment gets chaotic and you get bombarded with distractions. You'll be able to say no to distractions and remain focused on your priorities. Distractions will stand no chance of stopping you from achieving your vision of success. Also, you will be able to make quick decisions on what deserves your attention in the moment.

Step 3. Schedule Other Tasks

While your highest priorities should take up most of your workdays, there will also be other tasks that you need to complete. For these lesser-priority tasks, be sure to first ask, "Does this deserve my attention?" and then "How much and when?" Once you have those answers, schedule each task and give it your undivided attention.

Let's dive into what those lesser-priority tasks might be and how you can tackle them best:

- **Emails and other communication tools.** Emails need to be talked about first, because they take up so many hours in most professionals' days. They can also monopolize your days if you aren't careful. In order to ensure you don't spend too much of your day answering emails, intentionally decide how much attention your emails (and other ways of communicating) deserve, and schedule that time on your calendar accordingly. I suggest dividing that time into three to five chunks spread throughout your day. This allows you to be responsive to urgent requests while also accomplishing your priorities.

  It's incredibly important that you also evaluate the time you spend on emails and determine if you can find ways to get organized so you have fewer emails. You could talk to people that are sending you the most emails to figure out a win-win plan to reduce the emails back and forth.

  Keep in mind that most emails are less urgent than they appear and are more often than not someone else's priorities. So whenever possible, schedule time to handle emails. Respond to the urgent and important before the end of your business day; categorize the rest as nonurgent, and schedule time to deal with them accordingly.

- **Business needs.** Business needs such as filling out expense reports, creating or preparing for presentations, or organizing data should be scheduled so they don't fall through the cracks. Take the time now to brainstorm what would fall under this category so you can make sure everything is accounted for.

- **Research.** Many of us need to consume information online in order to improve our business outcomes. While this is true, it's also essential that you intentionally decide how much attention you want to allocate to such tasks. Not doing so could result in mindlessly falling into an online rabbit hole instead of getting the information you were looking for.

- **Planning for the unforeseen.** The reality is that you may not be able to accomplish everything you hoped in a day because of unforeseen circumstances, or your priorities may have to shift. That's OK, but in order to ensure you do get those tasks done in a timely manner, set aside 15 minutes at the end of each day to adjust your schedule for the next day.
- **Other tasks.** I suggest always having a list of tasks that you can work on if you find yourself with extra time in a day. This can be something like listening to a podcast, catching up on industry trends, enhancing a particular set of skills, etc. Over time, you'll get better at scheduling your priority-related tasks and find your equilibrium.

Trial and error over time will help you discover how much time you need to handle these other tasks, so be patient with yourself as you execute your Intentional Attention strategy.

Once you've got all your tasks scheduled, compartmentalize and give each task your best-quality undivided attention.

Reflection and Celebration

Schedule 30 minutes on your calendar every week for weekly reflection time. We'll be referring to this time in each of the following chapters. My reflection time is scheduled for every Sunday evening. I picked this day and time because it's when I feel most relaxed after the weekend and energized for the following week. Pick a time and day that works for you when you've got no other distractions. I suggest a time after your workweek has ended and before the next workweek starts.

During this time, look at your definitions of success and your priorities on your PSP. This will ensure you never lose sight of them. Then ask yourself, "Did I focus my attention on my highest priorities every day of last week?"

Were all my tasks worthy of my attention?

Did I move closer to my success in the most effective way?

Did I make the right decisions when priorities shifted in the moment?

If so, great. If not, that's OK, too. Don't be harsh on yourself. Just be sure you figure out what you could've done differently, learn from it, and course-correct. Then look at your calendar for the following week and ensure every day is structured around your highest priorities while also leaving room for the other, lesser priorities. Focus on progress and not on perfection. Be kind and compassionate with yourself. Remember, being intentional with your attention requires constant vigilance. If you need a reminder, put a calendar reminder to intentionally allocate your attention as often as needed.

After reflecting on your week, remember to celebrate every small success; this will energize you for the following week.

This time of reflecting and celebrating will help you master your strategy of Intentional Attention over time.

SET YOUR INTENTIONS

Promise yourself:
- My attention is my most valued, limited, and perishable asset.
- I will be intentional about what does and doesn't deserve my attention.
- I will structure each day around my highest priorities.

3

INTENTIONAL WORK-LIFE BALANCE

You can have it all. Just not all at once.
OPRAH WINFREY

THE THIRD strategy that will help you show your worth and emerge as a leader is Intentional Work-Life Balance, and in this chapter we will focus on how you intentionally thrive in your work and your life outside of work. Our jobs don't define us even if we love what we do. There's so much more to us than that. We're mothers, daughters, sisters, friends, volunteers, caregivers, and more. Each of our roles gives meaning to our lives, and all vie for our limited attention and energy.

Work-life balance means something different to everyone, but in essence, it's the state of equilibrium where a person prioritizes the demands of her career and the demands of her personal life. I've personally witnessed women's physical and mental health suffer as a result of letting the demands of work take over their lives. I've also seen women's careers suffer as they let the demands of their personal lives take over their careers. When you become intentional about balancing your work and life, you'll thrive in both.

———

My personal life almost ruined my professional life eight months after I got my first promotion to a sales leader when my husband left suddenly and unexpectedly. I was leading a team of 10 sales representatives and had a target of $120 million in sales. My team spanned the states of the Pacific Northwest: Washington, Oregon, Alaska, Utah, Montana, Nevada, and Idaho. My daughter, Sophia, was four, and my son, Samir, was two.

My world as I knew it fell apart, and I was devastated. Overnight, the intentional, energetic, proactive, optimistic, grateful, forward-moving Shelmina disappeared. She became an ashamed, angry, hurt, jealous, and betrayed woman. I was full of resentment and self-pity. My negative mental chatter was on overdrive. I was constantly distracted, overwhelmed, and preoccupied with anger and terror about my future and the future of my two young children.

I didn't sleep well, so I woke up tired every day. Exhausted, I woke up the kids, fed them breakfast, got them clean and dressed, rushed them to daycare, and sped off to work. I stopped making time for my old morning routine in order to fit in all the additional tasks I had to finish before I went to work. When I got to work, I was preoccupied, overwhelmed, and tired and was operating with the lowest levels of energy I'd ever experienced. My strategy of Intentional Attention went out the window. I couldn't focus my attention on anything. I'd sit through meetings in a daze and leave earlier than I used to because their dad used to pick them up from daycare and now that was my task. After picking up my children, I'd make dinner, clean, give baths, make lunches for the next day, read stories, get into bed exhausted, and still not sleep well. Then, I'd wake up even more tired the next day and do it all again. Up until then, my husband was my 50 percent partner in everything, and this change to 100 percent was incredibly hard.

My agitated mind was not capable of engaging effectively in any task—personal or professional. My negative mental chatter agonized about how broken homes produced damaged children. I was so shocked by what had gone wrong that I couldn't see a path forward. I had lost the ability to be present anywhere.

As hard as I tried to keep it all together, I couldn't. And my kids suffered the brunt of my anger. I was so frayed and on edge that the littlest things would set me off. Sophia had been especially close to her dad and drew pictures of him after he was gone, which made me feel terribly sorry for her and even more angry at him.

I lost control over my Power Quotient (which we'll dive deep into in Chapter 4). As first noted in Chapter 1, your PQ is your ability to scan your mental chatter and choose an empowering response to a disempowering stimulus. When you exercise your PQ, you intentionally choose your response. If you don't exercise your PQ, you give your power away to the stimulus by reacting to it. And at this point in my life, I was doing just that.

Days turned into weeks, and I wanted to put up a strong front, but not seeking support just made me crumble faster. I should have gone to see a therapist, but I didn't even know such people existed! I come from a culture and country where therapy isn't a thing.

After about five weeks of this misery, I was in a Friday afternoon meeting with my team and my boss. I was a zombie. Someone turned to me and asked for my perspective. I was startled: I hadn't been able to pay any attention during the entire meeting, and I had no idea what people had been talking about. I could barely understand the question.

I admitted that I was preoccupied with my personal situation and was not in a frame of mind to provide a concrete point of view. The people on my team were extremely understanding. I, however, felt terrible. They deserved a better leader. I decided I'd give up my leadership position, so at least if I failed at work, I'd only be letting myself down and not my entire team.

My stomach ached at the idea of giving up the leadership role I had worked so hard for, but it was what was best for the team. Or so I thought.

That Friday was a typical rainy Seattle day. On my way home, I got stuck in traffic and showed up late to pick up my children. The daycare provider was not happy, and her body language made that very clear, which made me more agitated. I complained all the way home.

Then, after we entered the house, the bulb in the light in the laundry room went out. My mental chatter got even worse: "Just what I need, one more task for me to do."

That evening, my children got into a small argument over dinner. I got angry at them and made both of them cry.

Instead of our usual nighttime reading, I decided we should go straight to sleep in the king-sized bed we shared. I was exhausted, and not in the mood to read a book.

After they fell asleep, I looked at their sad, innocent faces and felt terrible. My anger was spilling onto my children—the last thing I wanted.

I was failing as a mother as well as a leader. My children deserved better. My team deserved better.

> **INSIGHT**
>
> Stop squandering your precious attention on situations you can't control.

That night, I was even more restless than usual, and around 2 a.m., I went downstairs and sat on our living room floor with my head in my hands, feeling totally defeated. I kept repeating to myself: "I can't do this. I can't do this. I can't do this," while crying loudly. I cried and cried for hours until I could cry no more.

Until then, I'd kept it all bottled up inside: the grief over what happened to my marriage, my overwhelming sense of defeat, my exhaustion. I hadn't cried even once, because I didn't want to give my children the impression that I was weak and couldn't take care of them. I believed I needed to be their pillar of strength. They were dependent on me.

The more I cried, the lighter I felt. After hours of crying, I became still and sat there in total darkness and silence. It felt as if time had stopped, and my entire life flashed in front of me. I went back to my childhood and witnessed my incredible journey. Deep down, I began to realize just how lucky I was to have my two amazing children, a team that was understanding, and a career that I loved and that allowed me to raise my children as a single mother as well as support my parents financially. And I lived in a country in which I could do all this on my own.

> **INSIGHT**
>
> Your circumstances don't define you. Your responses do.

For the first time in weeks, I got a glimpse of my strong, resilient, grateful, eternally optimistic self, and it was as if I heard a voice from her: "You can do this. It will all work out." I felt these words in every core of my being, and it shifted my thinking from "I can't do this" *to* "I can do this." It was as if my old self were exercising her Power Quotient and reminding me of its power.

This became the turning point in my life and my career. I realized I had lost myself in my misery and let myself become a victim of my circumstances. I had forgotten to exercise my PQ to choose an empowering response to a disempowering stimulus.

My darkest night lifted into a beautiful new dawn. I knelt before the rising sun and prayed in extreme gratitude. It was Saturday morning. I crawled back into bed between my two children, kissed their cheeks, and immediately collapsed into a deep sleep.

I woke up with a renewed sense of hope. My situation hadn't changed, but I had changed. I knew from deep within me that I could handle my situation and everything would work out. My Power

Quotient enabled me to take my power back instead of giving it away to my circumstances.

That day we stayed in bed a little longer. We went out for breakfast. I watched Sophia and Samir play like they used to in the past. My children laughed, and their joy brought a smile to my face after a long, long time. Their laughter made my world right once again.

Later that day we hiked in the woods and went to the library. We were out all day enjoying ourselves. When we came home, I sat with them and watched their cartoons—I hadn't done that in weeks. Their eyes were on the TV screen and mine on them. Every time they laughed, I laughed with them.

That day also made me realize that I'd fallen into a "task trap" at home. I had a never-ending list of tasks to do. I was so busy moving from task to task that I'd forgotten to enjoy my time with my children: my most precious gifts and my highest priority.

That night I slept better than I had in a long time, and I woke up with slightly more energy on Sunday. Once again we stayed in bed a little longer and had a leisurely breakfast—no more rushing through the day. I cooked a few meals that would last us through the following week, and that day the process was actually enjoyable, as I was feeling better from within. I asked my children to help me with the cooking, which they were more than happy to do.

During my weekly reflection time that Sunday evening, I took extra time. I changed my definitions of success. I added the goal of achieving work-life balance to both my short- *and* long-term definitions of success because this balance would always be important, not just 12 months from that point. Before then, work-life balance was something *I did* but never actually *wrote down* as a definition of success. Once I wrote it down, it prompted me to apply the same level of discipline to it as I did to my other professional definitions of success.

I decided to apply my strategy of Intentional Attention to my time outside of work.

As I thought about everything I'd have to do to raise my children as a single mother, I did feel overwhelmed, but I used my PQ and shifted my narrative from "I *have* to do all this" to "I *get* to do all this," changing my situation from a *problem* to an *opportunity*. And raising my two children as a single mother proved to be an opportunity I'm forever grateful for.

I added my highest priorities outside of work to my PSP. I structured my time at home around my personal priorities just as I did my time at work around my professional priorities.

What I went through prompted me to prioritize my personal well-being, and that started by my scheduling "me time" every morning.

Each day I woke up 45 minutes before I woke up my children. I sat in silence for 15 minutes focusing on my breath, which was an enormous source of inner strength, calmness, and energy for me. I also made time for my previous morning ritual that included yoga stretches and sitting down to eat a healthy breakfast, and I actually started enjoying my masala chai, just as I used to.

> **INSIGHT**
>
> You never know how strong you are until you face challenges that force you to discover your hidden strength.

When I showed up to work that morning, I had more energy, and I could think more clearly. I could be more present. Many of my team members noticed me smile that day, and one even commented that I "looked good." I told them I felt better and thanked them for their patience and understanding. I promised myself to be more present and to do justice to my role as a leader.

Over the next several weeks, through many challenges, trials, errors, and lessons learned, I started to establish some semblance of work-life balance. I looked at every challenge as an opportunity to learn until I found that equilibrium where I could prioritize the demands of both my career and my personal life. And eventually, I found my rhythm and achieved levels of success I couldn't begin to dream of at the time.

A MINDSET FOR BALANCE

As my story illustrates, before you can even begin your journey to achieve a work-life balance, you must start with these three principles.

1. Believe Balance Is Possible

Achieving work-life balance begins with your mindset. Whatever you believe, you'll likely prove yourself right. You must know deep down in your core that balance is possible; otherwise you'll never achieve it. If you've got any doubts, you must work to shift your belief from "I can't" to "I can." Remember, your beliefs and your mental chatter are *yours*, and you can change them to whatever serves you well.

2. Nurture and Protect Your Inner Well-Being

If you want to succeed at work-life balance, you must make your inner well-being your number one priority, because as you read in my story, it impacts *everything*.

Your life and career are made up of a series of experiences. Each experience can be divided into two parts: the situation you're presented with *and* the way you respond to that situation. The situation is what it is, but the way you respond to that situation depends on how you view it, which in turn is dictated by your inner state. This means when you change your inner state, your response will change. That's how powerful your internal state is. It dictates whether you crumble, survive, or thrive. It impacts every choice you make, every experience you have, and every outcome you achieve. If your state of mind is negative, you'll likely look at everything through a negative lens. You'll be attracted to negativity—including negative thoughts, negative people, and negative information—all of which can pull you into a downward spiral. This negative inner state impacts your external interactions, too. Your misery will spill over on others, including those people you're closest to.

Your inner well-being also dictates your energy levels, so you must focus on what brings you joy and energizes you. Intentionally stay away from activities, people, and things that rob you of your joy and deplete your energy.

Some women think that prioritizing themselves and protecting their inner well-being is selfish and requires more time, but the reality is that prioritizing yourself and protecting your inner well-being is the most selfless thing you can do. Taking the time to prioritize your well-being will enable you to bring your best self to all our interactions so you will become more productive, energetic, and joyful in the office as well as beyond the office. Once you do this, you'll come to realize you can take on so much more in your life and your career than you ever have before.

3. Create a Narrative of Learning for Every Challenge

If you want to succeed at work-life balance, you must view every challenge as an opportunity to learn and grow.

The reality is that your life and career will hand you amazing highs, devastating lows, and everything in between. You don't get to choose what happens to you, but always remember you get to choose your response.

It's inevitable that you'll experience multiple personal and professional challenges throughout your career. Many career women encounter challenges not only in their job status, location, skill sets, or industry, but also in their personal lives, such as serious health issues, loss of loved ones, divorces, or care of sick family members. Such challenges are difficult and can feel overwhelming.

Take a break to recharge, reset, and seek help. Know that whatever challenge you're facing, it too shall pass. Everything passes. The key is not to let that challenge crumble you and create a downward spiral for everything else you've worked so hard to achieve in both your personal and professional life.

Navigating such challenges is tough, but it can be done with a learning mindset. Remember always that the challenge itself is not as important as the story you tell yourself about the challenge. Create a narrative that helps you learn and keeps you moving forward stronger and wiser.

INSIGHT

You can take the worst situation of your life and turn it into a narrative of learning.

Whenever you're faced with a challenge, ask yourself, "What can I learn from this?" Doing so will turn challenges into learning opportunities instead of problems that could weigh you down for an extended period of time. Remind yourself that you've faced challenges before and can do it again.

And if you make some mistakes, don't beat yourself up. Remember, this is hard and you're doing the best you can. Instead of regretting your mistakes or feeling guilty, learn from them so you don't make the same mistakes again. Be patient and be kind to yourself.

You'll have to try different things to find what works best for you. You can change your approach if it's not working for you.

Never give your power away to your challenges and become a victim. Exercise your PQ and choose an empowering response to every challenge, so you can learn and grow from it. As you learn from your challenges, you'll also become more resilient, stronger, and wiser. You'll learn to trust yourself to overcome whatever challenges come your way. Your self-trust will help you take chances on yourself. Also, just as professional challenges build your professional competence, your personal challenges will build character—and strong character matters more than anything else in the long run.

THE JOURNEY TO ACHIEVE WORK-LIFE BALANCE

With the mindset that work-life balance was possible, and with the determination to make my personal well-being my number one priority and view every challenge as an opportunity to learn, I started my journey toward achieving a work-life balance. The three basic principles that helped me were:

1. Determine personal priorities and schedule them.
2. Set boundaries.
3. Make intentional choices.

Let's walk through each of these steps.

1. Determine Personal Priorities and Schedule Them

I began to create and execute an Intentional Attention strategy for my hours outside of work. I started by determining my highest personal priorities. Next, I added them to my PSP and scheduled them on my calendar as far in advance as possible to ensure nothing important fell through the cracks and nothing insignificant took up my precious personal time.

I've worked with many women who don't set priorities for their life outside of work and find themselves exhausted by the activities that fill their personal time. It depletes them of their energy, which impacts their work performance.

When you structure your work life and your personal life around your priorities, both will energize you and bring you joy. Plus the energy and joy from your work life feeds your personal life and vice-versa. Sometimes the priorities overlap and you must choose what's a higher priority.

A case in point: My friend Erica Qualls-Beatty once told me about a day when her daughter looked at Erica's calendar and saw that her mom had noon blocked off on the same day that the daughter was receiving an award. She never told her mom about that ceremony because she saw her mom was busy. Luckily, the principal knew Erica well enough and told her about the ceremony, and she reworked her schedule to be there. The day of the ceremony, she sat in the audience with tears in her eyes as her daughter received recognition for all her hard work, and she realized a lesson so many of us need to learn: Your life is a whole, full life, and there are always roles that you play. You need to carve out time for those roles, because not only does that feed your soul, but it feeds the people around you.

Never feel like you have to say yes to things that don't line up with your priorities, both in and out of work. Schedule time for the people that matter, no matter the circumstance. They'll always be important to you.

2. Set Boundaries

Similar to my strategy of Intentional Attention at work, I had to learn to say no in order to set boundaries. As I navigated through my work-life balance journey, I realized the importance of setting two types of boundaries: one between my work hours and my nonwork hours so I could bring my best self to both, and the second within my personal nonwork hours.

On most days, I stopped working at 6 p.m. Everyone I worked with knew those were my boundaries, and my coworkers were respectful of that. I was a single mother, and my time with my children was just as important as my time at work. I was dedicated to my work during work hours. I was known to be a workaholic at work. After 6 p.m., I was equally dedicated to my life outside of work, which at that point was all about my children. Having such clear boundaries actually helped me be more productive at work: Knowing I had to stop at 6 p.m. made me exceptionally organized to ensure all urgent and important matters were taken care of before then. In the event that I had to make an exception due to a rare emergency that couldn't wait until the next morning or

> **INSIGHT**
>
> Value your energy and attention enough to set and stick to boundaries.

on days when I'd taken time during my workday to tend to personal priorities such as medical checkups or parent-teacher meetings, I finished my work after my children and I had dinner together or after they went to sleep.

I created a short evening routine to shift from "work mode" to "home mode" so I could be energized and completely present with my children. Just 10 minutes of a high-energy aerobic workout, changing out of my work clothes, and splashing cold water on my face created a shift in my mindset from work to home.

I set boundaries within my nonwork hours by saying no in a kind and gentle way to anything that vied for my attention which wasn't aligned with my highest personal priorities. When you know your priorities, it makes it easier for you to say yes to what matters the most and no to the rest—in the long term and in the moment.

This meant that I didn't accept every social invitation I received. I became very intentional about where, when, and to whom I gave my attention outside of work. Luckily, my family and friends were very understanding of this, too.

3. Make Intentional Choices

Another critical lesson I've learned is the importance of making intentional choices. These choices may be long term or short term, big or small, some in the moment, some easy and some very tough, but choices all the same.

No matter the situation, knowing my highest priorities, and understanding the trade-offs and consequences, made it easier to intentionally choose what was right for me.

Let me share a story to illustrate this point.

Six years after my personal crisis and continued achievements in my career, I was offered an incredible one-year growth opportunity to shadow Rodney Adkins (remember him from the Foreword?), who was leading a business in IBM's software group. This was an invitation-only role that was offered to IBM's top talent. It was an opportunity to gain exposure to and learn from Rod and all the other senior executives he interacted with. It also provided an incredible opportunity to watch how the most senior leaders operated and made decisions.

I was torn between keeping the children in their schools and accepting this opportunity since it required us to move to New York. This role would significantly improve my chances of getting promoted to an IBM executive.

Sophia was 11 years old, and Samir was 9.

I knew I'd have to travel extensively—both in the United States and internationally.

After much deliberation and discussion with mentors, I decided to talk to Rod to get his perspective. I told him about my desire to be promoted to an IBM executive position, and though that was very high on my list of priorities, my children were always my highest priority. Rod had witnessed my achievements and ambition for the past eight years.

Rod applauded me for prioritizing my children, as his family was also his priority. He assured me that if the role didn't work out, I could move back to Seattle whenever I chose. That sealed my decision.

We moved to Katonah, New York, in the summer of 2002. I hired a woman named Gail to stay with us Monday morning through Friday evening. She attended college near our house, and her own home was 1½ hours away, so the arrangement met everyone's needs perfectly.

Two weeks after I moved, I joined Rod in IBM's corporate jet to Austin, Texas, for a town hall meeting with all the employees and some one-on-one meetings with Rod's mentees. I was excited to experience the corporate jet travel I'd heard so much about. About 3½ hours after takeoff, we landed in Austin. At the time, there was no internet service on flights. As soon as we landed, I turned on my phone. I had received a phone call and an email from my son's school. The two messages shared that Samir had a fever and was being isolated in the nurse's room and that I should pick him up as soon as possible. It was 8:30 a.m. in Austin and 9:30 a.m. in Katonah.

My mental chatter started going crazy: "This has never happened before. Why does it have to happen today? Rod will think I'm not capable of becoming an IBM executive because I could have unexpected children's emergencies. If this had happened in Seattle, I could've called someone to help me, but I don't know anyone in Katonah, and Gail is at school."

After the first few minutes of turbulence in my mind, I took a deep breath and used my PQ to scan my mental chatter so I could choose an empowering response.

"What deserves my attention *now*?" I asked myself. The answer was very clear.

My children were my top priority, and my child was sick. My son needed me, so I must go get him. If this meant Rod didn't think I could be an IBM executive, so be it. My son's health was my priority, and I was willing to accept the consequences of my decision. This felt freeing and gave me the confidence to approach Rod. I made an intentional choice, and I understood the trade-offs.

"I have a situation with Samir that requires me to be back in Katonah as soon as possible," I shared with Rod.

> **INSIGHT**
>
> When your priorities are clear, you can make better decisions about what deserves your attention—both long-term and in the moment.

He didn't seem fazed at all. Instead, he asked, "What happened to Samir?"

I explained what was going on, and I was pleasantly surprised by his response. Rod had moved from Austin to New York and knew exactly when the next flight from Austin to White Plains was. He said, "There's a flight leaving Austin at 9:25 a.m. that will get you to White Plains before 2 p.m. If he needs to be picked up prior to that, we can have someone in the office help."

My respect for Rod went through the roof. I made a mental note: "What an incredible leader! I want to be like him."

I called the school and explained my situation. The person I spoke to said the fever was mild, so my son could remain in the nurse's room until I arrived. I picked him up a few hours before school ended.

Samir was fine by the evening, and life was back to normal the very next day.

Each one of us has different circumstances, sets of choices, and trade-offs that work for us. Your choices and trade-offs should enable you to thrive in both your work and your personal life. Sometimes work wins, and sometimes life wins. As long as you make decisions with your priorities, trade-offs, and consequences in mind, your choices will be right for you.

My quest to achieve a good work-life balance also taught me invaluable skills such as patience, forgiveness, letting go, and self-trust which improved my ability to achieve success at work. Creating and executing the strategy of Intentional Attention at home strengthened my strategy at work, and as a result, not only did I achieve my short-term definition of success; I also achieved one of my long-term definitions of success in just two years after my personal crisis instead of five. I was promoted to a second line sales leader. This position meant I had the opportunity to lead a team of 7 sales leaders and 150 salespeople all with a target of generating $950 million in revenue annually all while my children continued to be the source of my inspiration, strength, and joy and the fuel for my success at work.

As my children grew up and my career was also on the rise, everything around me was in constant flux. However, these three guiding principles helped me achieve a work-life balance and thrive in both.

A STORY OF INTENTIONAL WORK-LIFE BALANCE

Priscilla Eun-Young Abji
Owner, PAC Services

Many women believe they must choose between their career and their children, especially when their children need extra support. Priscilla Eun-Young Abji is a Korean American, a therapist, and a mother of two children, and I also happen to be related to her by marriage. In her story, she shares her struggles and how she found work-life balance through the challenges of motherhood.

In my early twenties, I had a vision of how my life would play out. I proudly announced that I didn't want to get married or have biological kids. I had a passion for underserved youth, especially those who struggled with anger and violent tendencies. In pursuit of my passion, I completed my master's in urban education at UCLA and began my first career as a high school teacher in South Central LA. It was a dream come true. I loved my job and my students. However, upon discovering the mental health needs in the community, I pursued a master's in social work at USC, and I started my second career as a social worker/clinical therapist. I also consistently sought out volunteer opportunities where I could spend my evenings and weekends working with teens on probation, in the foster system, involved in gangs, and/or struggling with housing. By the time I was 23, I also had applications and agencies bookmarked for my plan to adopt a teenage girl through the foster system, envisioning a future of the two of us against the world. This dream was my life and heart's commitment. I felt so sure of who I was and where I was going.

Then, I met my husband, I fell in love, and the next thing you know, I said yes to his proposal. After softening my heart to the idea of sharing love and a life with someone, I started to understand the pull to have children with someone you love. Shortly after, my daughter, Aleela, was born. I was positively smitten. I loved her so much I felt my heart could barely contain it.

But here's the twist. Although I loved my family beyond words, I experienced an internal struggle alongside the joys of motherhood. I faced doubts and waves of identity crisis. So much of my identity, life goals, and dreams had been around being this independent career woman completely dedicated to the youth I worked with. I had childcare set up to begin immediately after my three-month maternity leave and didn't foresee motherhood impeding much on my career. However, the very week I was supposed to return to work full-time, my baby decided to refuse milk unless it was directly from the breast. We tried different types and temperatures of milk, endless bottles and nipples, and various methods of feeding including finger feeding, an SNS feeding tube, straws, a syringe, and even a shot glass. We tried every method we could, but I had given birth to one strong-willed baby. She only wanted to feed at the breast, and there were no ifs, ands, or buts about it. I had to make a choice. After many tears, I reluctantly resigned from my job and faced the possibility that my career goals may not be compatible with my new life.

I felt lost and afraid of what this detour might mean for me and my career. Never did I doubt that my daughter was worth anything and everything, but so much of this hadn't been on my terms. Since my first job in tenth grade, I had never had a gap in employment, so working was a huge part of my identity and the main channel to accomplish my bigger life goals. What was especially difficult was being only three months short of completing my licensing hours, which I needed to do in order to take my licensing exam. I had already felt delayed by my maternity leave and was eager to get back on track. Yet here I was, straying further off track.

A few months later, my daughter finally decided to drink milk from a cup with a straw (aka a sippy cup), and that very night, I started job searching. By then, I realized that even when I returned to work, all those late hours I used to pour into my job and volunteer work weren't going to be as easy to come by. Coming home past 9 p.m. three nights in a row, dedicating weekends to volunteer events, and fielding the occasional late-night emergencies wasn't realistic for my life as a mom of an infant. I had also started to experience the benefits that can come with being a stay-at-home mom and wasn't sure if I wanted to completely let all that go. I had to redefine what work-life balance meant to me. So after more tears and contemplation, I decided to take two part-time jobs that would allow me the flexibility to remain a stay-at-home mom.

The first job was as a clinical therapist, where I scheduled my clients around my daughter's sleep times and my husband's work schedule. The other was as a weekend social worker at a psychiatric hospital. Balancing taking care of an infant full-time with two part-time jobs left minimal time for anything else. There were moments when the only thing I dreamed of was sleep and a shower, sometimes making me wonder if I had any passion left for my career. Those were scary moments for me. I even tested myself by trying things that would normally get me passionate to see if the spark was still there, all while I watched my colleagues complete their hours, pass their licensing exams, receive promotions, start their own practices, casually have time to socialize after work, attend networking events without a second thought, and make big steps in their career. I grew frustrated over my career's slow progress due to my split responsibilities and my part-time pace. Maintaining a healthy balance between my career, child, husband, and myself felt near impossible.

Here's where the second twist comes in. Around the time my daughter was a year old, I began to release my need for control—sometimes out of wisdom and sometimes out of exhaustion. I acknowledged and processed through my resentment, loss, frustration, sadness, and anger instead of trying to fight it or cover it up. I stopped living in what "should have been" and opened my eyes to what was in front of me. I actively worked hard to be present, initially for my child, but it in turn impacted my ability to be present as a whole. I gained clarity on my priorities, and it helped me set boundaries with more confidence. I started to grasp the reality that instead of continuing to pit one part of my life against the other, I could allow for them to contribute toward each other. The feeling of powerlessness began to lift, and gratitude and excitement filled its place. In this new space, I realized that the part-time positions that I thought were delaying me actually set me up on a faster track to starting my own practice than if I had stayed at my previous job. I saw that without my reluctant resignation, I wouldn't have been pushed to find the jobs that ended up being better aligned with my career goals. The time that I thought I was losing ended up being much needed time that allowed me to reflect, renew, and develop a clearer focus on how my identity and career intersected.

Motherhood taught me more about myself than any other life experience, and it was a catalyst for exponential growth. Bringing that new version of me into my work took it to another level I couldn't have incorporated into my previous goals because I hadn't even known it existed. Every step I'd perceived as a step back turned out to be a step forward. Motherhood hadn't been a detour. On the contrary, my new identity and the journey it took me on turned out to be one of the most valuable assets to my career. I'll forever be thankful to my family for that.

With this renewed mindset, I completed my licensing hours. While 29 weeks pregnant with my second child, Axton, I sat, Braxton-Hicks contractions and all, and took my licensing exam and passed it. When Axton was eight months old, I successfully opened my own practice, and with it came big and bold dreams for its future. I'm still limiting my hours so I can be a stay-at-home mom until the kids are school-aged. However, this time, I have peace and excitement for how my long-term goals will continue to evolve in the years to come and with every new life stage. I've learned to harness the power that comes through translating deferred dreams to opportunities instead of barriers. I've learned that having a successful work-life balance doesn't mean having a perfect formula figured out; it means to practice the arts of fluidity, adaptability, and acceptance. I can now confidently say that my motherhood journey has actually made room for my dreams to get bigger, not smaller. Finding this balance didn't come easy, and it definitely requires continual reflection and maintenance. It's an ongoing journey. But it's one I now look forward to and am proud to model for my children, Aleela and Axton, the next generation.

INTENTIONAL EXERCISES

Before we can really dive into the specifics for how you can create and execute your work-life balance strategy, it's essential that you're able to answer yes to the following questions:

- Do I believe I can achieve work-life balance?
- Can I make my inner well-being my top priority?
- Can I view challenges as an opportunity to learn and grow?

If a no even creeped up in your mind, examine your self-limiting beliefs that are preventing you from that yes. Know that your beliefs are *yours*, and you own the power to choose what you believe. Shift your beliefs until you can sincerely say "Yes" to all three.

Once you are able to say yes to all three of these questions without a doubt, you're ready to start creating and executing your Intentional Work-Life Balance strategy.

Introspection

Let's start by answering the following questions to gain self-knowledge and get a better understanding of your current state of work-life balance:

Life Audit
- Do I have a morning routine? Does this routine energize me?
- Do I eat healthy, well-balanced meals? Do I eat these meals in a hurry, or do I take the time to enjoy my food?
- Do I have an evening routine to transition from work to life activities?
- How much sleep do I get each night? Is that the right amount of sleep I should be getting?
- Do I have a bedtime routine? If not, do I need to create one to help me get settled and ready for a good night of sleep?
- Who or what in my personal life brings me a tremendous amount of energy or joy?
- What activities do I perform outside of work? Do these activities energize me?
- What do I feed my mind outside of work? (Think social media, news, television, books, classes, etc.) How much time do I spend with this content? Does it energize me?
- Am I inadvertently giving my power to another person or situation in my personal life?

- If so, who or what is taking that power away?
- What's currently causing me stress, imbalance, or dissatisfaction outside of work?
- What am I prioritizing—consciously and unconsciously—in my personal life?
- What can I outsource to free up my precious and limited personal time (for example, house cleaning, laundry, yard work, etc.)?

Work Audit

- How are my energy levels when I begin my workday?
- How are my energy levels in the middle of my workday?
- How are my energy levels when I end my workday?
- When do I start and end my workday?
- Who or what in my professional life brings me a tremendous amount of energy or joy?
- Who or what in my professional life depletes my energy or joy?
- What's currently causing me stress, imbalance, or dissatisfaction at work?
- Am I inadvertently giving my power to another person or situation in my professional life?
- If so, who or what is taking that power away?
- Do I need to create a transition ritual at the end of my workday that allows me to completely unplug from work and be fully present after I leave the office?

Application

Now that you have a better understanding of where you stand with your current work-life balance, let's focus on applying the insights you learned in this chapter to create and execute your strategy of Intentional Work-Life Balance.

A good work-life balance will immediately provide numerous benefits, including less stress, a lower risk of burnout, a greater sense of well-being, improved productivity, and higher engagement at work.

First, determine why "achieving work-life balance" should be one of your definitions of success. Some examples of this include "so I can maximize my potential both personally and professionally," "so I can thrive in all areas of my life," and "so I can spend quality time with my family/run a marathon/read more books/etc."

Next, add "Achieve work-life balance" to both your short- and long-term definitions of success.

Determine Personal Priorities and Schedule Them

Determine your highest priorities outside of work and add them to your PSP. Be sure this includes nurturing and protecting your inner well-being, because without that, you won't have a foundation for long-term sustainable success. Remember, jobs will come and go, but once your health or personal relationships suffer, you might not be able to recover.

To determine your personal well-being priorities, ask yourself this question: "What's the one thing I can do that will improve my _____ well-being right now?" You can fill in the blank with "physical," "mental," "emotional," or whatever part of your life you choose to prioritize.

For example, you can ask, "What's the one thing I can do to improve my *physical* well-being right now?" Your answers to this could be:

- Sleep more.
- Eat a more well-balanced diet.
- Work out for 30 minutes, four times a week.

You could also ask, "What's the one thing I can do to improve my *mental* well-being right now?" Some answers to this question could be:

- Make time for relationships that are important for me.
- Call someone I respect and admire once a week.
- Take a yearly vacation.
- Get a weekly or biweekly massage.
- Create a morning routine that includes meditation and/or yoga.
- Create time for an evening routine.

Once you've determined your personal well-being priorities, schedule them on your calendar. Next, determine all your other highest personal priorities and schedule them. These can include important birthdays, anniversaries, weddings, religious holidays, health checkups, etc. Then, schedule activities that bring you joy, energize you, inspire you, and bring out the best in you.

When you structure your hours outside of work around your personal priorities, you'll feel a sense of inner success and fulfillment. You'll feel energized and joyful, both of which will stay with you everywhere you go, including at the office.

Set Boundaries

Setting boundaries between your personal and professional life is necessary if you want to thrive in both. Just as your work deserves your full attention, so does your personal life. If you don't set boundaries for yourself—and actually respect them—no one else will. While setting them in the first place might be difficult, it will get easier over time, and others will come to respect your boundaries.

Boundary 1: Work and Nonwork Hours

When you don't set boundaries, not only will your productivity suffer and your performance impacted, but you'll also run the risk of burning out. Not setting boundaries hurts not only you, but also your family, your friends, and your work.

Keeping in mind that your achievement at work is tied to your productivity and not based on the number of hours you work. Start by determining your work hours, that will enable you to thrive at work and outside of work, and enable you to have a good work-life balance. For some people, that means working eight hours a day, and for others it means longer. I recommend no more than nine hours a day so your productivity levels remain at their highest.

Once you've set your schedule, be consistent and respect it yourself. If you don't, no one will take you seriously. Set expectations, and let everyone you work with know your work hours so they will respect them. When you make an exception, let people know you're making an exception and tell them why. Make those exceptions rare and only when truly needed.

Also be sure not to let life activities encroach on your work hours unless you have a personal priority that is higher than your work priority like a health checkup already scheduled or there's an emergency. Let your family and friends know about your boundaries so they'll respect them. Honor those boundaries by not taking personal calls when you're at work. Let calls go into your voice mail, and return calls after you're done working.

When you're at home, give your full attention to your personal life; and when you're at work, give your full attention to your work.

Boundary 2: Within Your Nonwork Hours

In order to make the most of your nonwork hours, you must also set boundaries for nonwork-related activities. You only have so much time outside of work, and that time is both precious and perishable.

In the last chapter we learned to set boundaries at work by saying no to things that aren't worthy of your attention at work. The same principle applies to your nonwork hours.

Once you've prioritized what things are important and scheduled time for them on your calendar, say no to what is not worthy of your limited energy and attention outside of work.

When saying no, keep in mind that your personal relationships are important and will outlast your professional relationships, so be sincere and tell your family and friends why you must decline their invitation.

Also say no to anything that depletes you of your energy or your joy, like watching negative news or endlessly scrolling on social media. If you intentionally choose to spend your time on such activities, decide in advance just how much and stick to it.

Make Intentional Choices

Your work-life balance is a reflection of all the choices you make—long term and short term, big and small, tough and easy. Make those choices intentionally by knowing your priorities, acknowledging the trade-offs you're willing to make, and understanding the consequences of your choices.

Remember that your choices need to be right for you and those directly impacted by your decision only. Never make your decisions based on others' expectations or opinions. This is *your* life, and your choices are yours alone, so make them on your own terms.

Choosing between work and life will be hard at times, and there will be some days you question your choice. When that does happen, gently remind yourself why you made that decision and why it's the right decision for you. Owning your choices doesn't mean sticking with them forever either. Change when you need to, and don't be harsh with yourself if you make mistakes. Instead, be grateful that you now have the insights to make better choices in the future.

Reflection and Celebration

During your weekly reflection time, focus on your week both at work and outside of work, and ask yourself these questions:

- Did I balance my work and my life well?
- Did my career overtake my personal demands?
- Did my personal demands overtake my career?
- What changes do I need to make next week so I can prioritize both my work and my life?

Reflect, learn, and course-correct as necessary. Focus on progress and not on perfection. Remember, balancing work and life is hard work and requires constant vigilance. If you need a reminder, put a calendar reminder to intentionally balance your work and life as often as needed.

Make sure to celebrate small victories—no matter how small they are—and be grateful that you get to thrive in both areas, as that will energize you to keep maintaining your work-life balance while everything around you is in constant flux.

SET YOUR INTENTIONS

Promise yourself:
- I will thrive in both my personal and professional life.
- I will prioritize my personal well-being so I can bring my best self to my work as well as to my life outside of work.
- I will never become a victim of my circumstances.

4

INTENTIONAL VALUE CREATION

*When you undervalue what you do,
the world will undervalue who you are.*
OPRAH WINFREY

THE FOURTH strategy that will help you show your worth and emerge as a leader is Intentional Value Creation. Your worth to your organization is tightly coupled with the value you create. The higher the value you create, the higher your worth. You were hired to create a certain amount of value for your organization, you keep your job because you create that value, and you progress in your career when the value you create exceeds what's expected of you. At our hectic pace, if we're not intentional about creating value, we tend to run on autopilot. We often don't see what's really needed of us, we may not appreciate the impact we have, and we may not be aware of the unique ways we can create value.

In Chapter 2, "Intentional Attention," you scheduled tasks/meetings/activities on your calendar that give you the best chance of achieving your success. In this chapter we'll talk about how you can accelerate your success by intentionally creating value at your maximum capacity in all your interactions whether they are one-on-one conversation, group conversation (including email and other forms of electronic communications), or meeting in person or virtually.

When you show up to work every day with the intention of creating value at your maximum capacity in every interaction, the value you'll contribute will surpass all expectations and become a game changer for your career. Your value contribution will be reflected in your performance, your worth to your organization, and the achievement of your short-term vision of success. In addition to the value you create for your own success, seek to create value for the success of your stakeholders including your peers, clients, boss and your entire organization.

The higher and the more unique your value, the harder it is for anyone else to replicate your value or replace you. You become essential to the success of your organization. For any leader, it's always clear which employees are most essential to the leader's success and the success of the organization as a whole. Retaining these employees is a key priority. They're the ones getting promotions, stock options, higher salary increases, awards, and more. When they want something—a growth assignment, flexible hours, time off, etc.—they're in a position of power to negotiate because their company needs them just as much as if not more than they need the company. Such is the power of the value you create for your organization.

With all of that being said, as an underrepresented minority, I know firsthand that there are many internal and external barriers that could potentially sabotage your ability to contribute value at your maximum capacity, and we'll work together to tackle those in this chapter.

When I started my career, I allowed my internal barriers to sabotage my ability to create value at my maximum capacity. As I shared earlier, my first job out of college was as a software developer at ETA Systems with a salary that allowed me to lift my family out of poverty.

I was excited to start my job. At first, I went to work every day with a spring in my step and poured my heart into my work. I was living the dream, and I was deeply aware of how lucky I was. Soon I found myself, like many other women in the technology field, the only woman or one of the very few in every room. Meeting after meeting, memo after memo, I began to realize that none of my coworkers looked like me or spoke like me. They had degrees from well-recognized and even Ivy League colleges. Many of them boasted master's degrees and PhDs. They were all more experienced and more credentialed than I was and had bigger titles. I started comparing myself with them and convinced myself there was nothing I knew that they didn't already know. I started to wonder if I belonged there. This put me in a pattern of undermining my own capabilities and underestimating my worth.

I did a good job on my own projects, but whenever I had an idea in meetings, I was afraid to speak up. I was worried that I'd sound stupid and believed that *my ideas didn't matter.* That fear, in its desire to protect me, told me it was safer to stay quiet. To make matters worse, I was on a one-year work visa, and if my company chose not to extend it, I'd have to go back to Tanzania where there were no computer science jobs and everything my parents and I had worked so hard for would be ruined. My dream of lifting my family and myself out of poverty would be very short-lived.

Three months passed, and one Tuesday afternoon, my coworkers, our bosses, and I were discussing an urgent problem with testing our software, and I had a great idea—a *really* great idea.

Fear's voice was resounding loudly in my head, telling me if I spoke up, I might sound ridiculous and my bosses might realize that they'd made a mistake in hiring me. Perhaps they'd even fire me.

So I didn't say anything.

And then as if the idea jumped from my brain and into the brain of my colleague sitting across from me, he said exactly what I'd been thinking. His idea sparked the eureka moment that changed the team's testing approach entirely.

Stunned, I watched the room light up with enthusiasm. Our bosses were impressed. They patted my coworker on his back and talked about how his idea was so unique and solved a critical problem for the entire organization.

When the meeting ended, I left the conference room and retreated to the bathroom. I looked at myself in the mirror and silently chastised myself: "You should've spoken up! That could've been you! You have unique ideas that can solve critical problems for your entire organization."

I was young, new, and insecure, but somehow seeing my idea voiced by someone else, and praised, felt like a validation of my capabilities. A moment later, while still staring at my reflection, it hit me. I thought: "It doesn't matter that I'm a woman of color, what my accent is, what university I went to, what level of education I have, or how young I am. I have unique perspectives and problem-solving capabilities that can create value for my entire organization. *My ideas do matter!*"

That experience taught me a powerful lesson that I could change my own beliefs.

That change in my belief from "My ideas don't matter" to "My ideas do matter" was the inner victory I needed before I could have any external victories.

A few days later, sitting in a meeting, I had another great idea. Once again, fear showed up as a loud voice in my head telling me all the same old things about what could go wrong if I spoke up. But this time, another voice whispered to me as well, a voice I hadn't heard in a very long time: my voice of courage, fueled by my new belief that my ideas mattered. It told me about all the things that could go *right* if I spoke up. "This is my opportunity," I told myself, "to show them I have great ideas that can create unique value. Take this chance! If they like my idea, they'll extend my visa past the one year. They might even sponsor me for a green card, and I'll be able to keep my dream alive by working in the United States of America! My family and I will never have to be poor again." (This is a great example of why defining success is so critical. *The possibility of keeping my dream alive was the best motivation in the world.*)

Sitting in that meeting, witnessing this debate in my head about whether to speak up or not, I realized that fear and courage were *voices in my head*, but they were not *me*. I could intervene and manage these voices. I had the power to determine who won this debate. I spoke to my voice of fear: "Fear, I hear you loud and clear. I know you mean well and are trying to protect me. But this time I won't let you stop me. The rewards of speaking up are life changing. I must take this chance."

And then I spoke up.

All eyes turned to me. None of them had heard me speak at a meeting before. In fact, I imagine many of them had never heard any woman of color speak up at a meeting, as I was the only one in our department.

Of course, in that moment, the fear didn't go away. My voice trembled; my stomach tightened; my heart raced. I didn't take a single breath until I finished expressing my idea. But as soon as it had leaped from my mouth into the air, I felt as if a hundred-pound boulder had been lifted off my chest.

My idea was well received, and I was the one getting the pat on the back that day. For the first time since I started my job, I realized I had contributed value that was beyond my project. I had influenced the direction and success of my company! After the meeting, colleagues who didn't normally speak to me approached me to let me know what a great idea I had. I was creating value, and it was being noticed.

That tiny moment taught me a powerful lesson: I owned the power to manage the voices in my head and intentionally choose an empowering response. This was the day I coined the term "Power Quotient."

As noted earlier in the book, your Power Quotient (PQ) is your ability to scan your mental chatter and intentionally choose an empowering response to a disempowering stimulus. In this case, the disempowering stimulus was my own voice of fear.

Prior to this moment, I'd unconsciously exercised my PQ many times in my life (remember the time when I almost left college?). But now I was intentionally choosing an empowering response. I was finally aware of the enormous power I owned over the voices in my head.

When you exercise your PQ, you never give your power away to any stimulus; you own it by intentionally choosing your response. However, as I noted in the last chapter, just because I became aware of my PQ didn't mean it was easy to exercise it all the time. But the more you do it, the better you get at it.

VALUE CREATION BARRIERS

I have worked with many women who face similar barriers to value creation as I did. They too are discouraged by not seeing enough people in the room who look like them, who are relatable to their race, sex, education level, or cultural and socioeconomic backgrounds. It all starts with internalizing and using your competence to create value in all your interactions.

Now, let's address internal and external barriers many of us face so we can dismantle them and create value at our maximum capacity. The key is to recognize your own value and know your worth. It is only when you know your worth that you can show your worth. You can show our worth to everyone you interact with.

Your "Unders"

As my story illustrated, I overhyped and overemphasized my "unders"—I felt like an *under*represented woman in a male-dominated field. *Under*educated compared with the others, *under*privileged in my economic status, and *under*proficient in the language and culture. And the worst part of those unders was that they caused me to believe, think, and act *under*. I undermined my capabilities, undervalued my opinions, and underestimated my worth.

> **INSIGHT**
>
> If you allow your "unders" to have the upper hand, you will not emerge as a leader.

My unders were just figments of my confused and insecure imagination, but at the time, they seemed very real and extremely threatening. If I hadn't had that moment of truth while looking in the mirror on that bleak day—a day I now consider a blessing—my unders would've kept the upper hand, and I wouldn't be here today writing this book.

Many of us get focused on our unders, which causes us to undermine our capabilities, and we must change that. Don't get caught up in your unders and give them the upper hand. Emerge from your "unders" by internalizing your competence, valuing your opinions, and knowing your worth. Change your beliefs as I did. Your beliefs are your beliefs, and you can change them as you wish. You must recognize your own capabilities before you can create value with them. Your capabilities will lie dormant within you if you let your unders keep the upper hand. With this newfound awareness, begin to watch your behavior and determine which unders are stopping you from contributing value at your maximum capacity and become stubbornly determined to emerge from every single one of them.

Workplace Fears

Oftentimes, even after we recognize our capabilities, our fear will stop many of us from contributing value at our maximum capacity. Whenever you're fearful, you shortchange your ability to create value.

In addition to speaking up, other common fears that women face in the workplace include being judged, failing, not being liked, drawing negative attention, seeming overly ambitious, and disappointing others. Fear is a state of mind perpetuated by your negative mental chatter.

Typically, when your voice of fear shows up to protect you, it says something like, "Don't do this; it won't work out." Remember that you don't have to give into fear. You can intentionally engage your voice of courage and ask instead, "What if it does work out?" You can amplify your voice of courage by giving it reasons why you must contribute value, and you can use your PQ to scan your mental chatter and choose a response of courage.

The more you do this, the better you get at it. Over time, fear's grip over you will loosen and your voice of courage will get stronger.

Past Programming

Another barrier that stops women from contributing value at their maximum capacity is their past programming, which they may or may not even be aware of. Many women I've worked with have been taught at a young age that "girls are to be seen and not heard," especially around elders. These same women often struggle to speak up in the presence of people that are more senior to them—in title or age. Some are taught to conform, and because of this, they struggle to express points of view that differ from that of their leaders.

I mentored an exceptionally smart software engineer in her midtwenties who had approached me after listening to my talk at a conference. She worked for a large technology company and was having difficulty speaking up during meetings with her boss. I shared my story from earlier in this chapter about my struggle to speak up and explained how I changed my beliefs and exercised my PQ to speak up. She promised she would try that.

A couple of months later, we met again. Shortly after we sat down, she started to cry. She told me, "I can't speak up regardless of how hard I try. I tried using my Power Quotient to shift my thoughts, but the voices in my head are too loud, and they keep repeating, 'You're not smart enough, and your ideas aren't good enough.' And of course, someone else suggested the same idea that I was too scared to suggest, and it caught fire! He was not only recognized by our general manager; he even got promoted. He's a really nice guy, and I'm happy for him, but I can't seem to get out of my own way."

Her hands were shaking, and her face was covered in tears, so I decided to shift the conversation away from work until she could calm down a little. We talked about our families instead. She came from an Indian family in which everyone was educated and accomplished. Both her parents had PhDs. She had two older brothers with PhDs. "I'm the dumbest of them all," she lamented. "I'm the only one with only a master's degree. Every time we have a debate at dinner, I lose, so I just stay out of it."

She admired and respected her family but didn't realize that in the process of comparing herself with them, she had undermined her own talent and conditioned herself to think that she wasn't smart enough from a very young age.

I knew this belief was stopping her from speaking up. I also realized that it wasn't easy for her to change her belief just because I suggested it, so I tried a different approach

Our backgrounds were very different, but she was a programmer and I had been one in the past, so I decided to use a software analogy. I compared the way we operate with the way a computer program works. I explained that our experiences create the program by which we operate. In some experiences, we're active participants; in others, we aren't. Either way, the program is being written, and it controls how we operate—until we decide to change it.

Her eyes lit up.

"When we become conscious of our program," I explained, "we can recognize what programming hasn't been serving us and rewrite our program."

She chimed in, "We can debug our own program!" We had both been test engineers and had spent hours finding bugs in programs, so she saw where I was going. We both laughed. Then she said, "I need to debug the program of thinking that I'm not smart enough."

When we met a month later, she was smiling from ear to ear. Her first words when I saw her were: "I've become the author of my programming, and you won't believe this! Not only am I speaking up in meetings; I'm finding and removing all kinds of bugs from my programming . . . and I'm also installing new features—like making time to take care of myself!"

All of us are programmed by our life experiences, which instill certain beliefs. These beliefs are so deeply ingrained in us that we can't easily change them by sheer will. It takes real, deep effort and different approaches to change them.

You're the author of your own programming, and while your past may currently be sabotaging your ability to create value at your maximum capacity, you can rewrite your own program and instill new beliefs.

From this day forward, become aware of your past conditioning and determine which self-limiting beliefs are stopping you from creating maximum value; then reprogram yourself to change your beliefs.

Communication Skills

Communicating effectively is a critical skill when it comes to creating value for your own projects and those outside your immediate project.

It doesn't matter how great your ideas are inside your head; if you can't articulate them so they can be heard and understood clearly, you can't create value for others.

This was something I struggled with early on in my career. Once I overcame my fear of speaking up, I realized that I had a tendency to ramble when I was explaining my ideas, and I could see folks "zoning out" as I spoke. I quickly realized I had to learn how to speak in a way that would ensure I was heard and understood.

I began to observe and learn from the most effective speakers— the ones who command pin-drop silence whenever they speak. I learned how they stated their ideas clearly and concisely. How they spoke with the right energy level—not too loud, not too soft, not too fast, not too slow. How their words reflected confidence in themselves and their ideas.

I learned to be clear and concise by writing and rewriting my ideas before I spoke up. I visualized myself speaking with the right energy level, the right tone, the right pace.

Word Choice

Another barrier to creating maximum value is the wrong choice of words. I used to inadvertently undermine my own idea before I even stated it, opening with words like "I'm sorry, but...," or "I *just* wanted to say...," or "I'm no expert but..."

> **INSIGHT**
>
> How you express your idea determines how it's received.

I realized that when I wasn't expressing confidence in my own ideas, no one else had confidence in them, and so I learned to pick my words with intention. I eliminated words like "sorry" and "just" when I presented my ideas. I also learned never to use phrases such as "I'm not sure but..." or "This might sound stupid/weird/strange but..." Always express your ideas with words that convey confidence. Saying "I believe" versus "I think" conveys strength and assurance in your words. If you don't have confidence in your ideas, you can't expect anyone else to have confidence in them either.

Many women I work with say "sorry" constantly, even when it's not at all necessary. Oftentimes, when I'm speaking at a conference, I grab a drink of water from the fountain, and many times I have to wait for a woman in front of me to finish. Too many times, the woman in front of me will stop drinking and say "I'm sorry." I always ask "For what," and the answer is almost always "Because I made you wait." And my response is always the same: "You didn't make me wait. I came after you and should have to wait my turn." This conversation has made me some lifelong friends and made others realize how our words can undermine us—in even the smallest of instances.

> **INSIGHT**
>
> Apologizing when needed is a sign of strength. Apologizing all the time strips your sorry of its meaning.

There's a difference between taking responsibility and apologizing constantly, which I did, and many other women do (at the water fountain and beyond!). When you apologize too often, you weaken the power of your apologies. And when you're in front of certain audiences, you could come across as weak. Apologize only when you should. When your apologies are infrequent and sincere, they'll carry more weight.

After stating an idea, never ask if what you said makes sense. Doing so portrays a lack of confidence in your own idea. Instead, ask, "What's your perspective?" or "What are your thoughts?"

Just as the wrong choice of words can dilute your effectiveness, the right choice of words can enhance your effectiveness and confidence. They can show care and respect, establish rapport, build relationships, and earn the trust and confidence of others—all of which are critical for you to contribute value.

Interruptions

Another barrier I had to deal with, and many other women I have worked with also have had to deal with, is getting interrupted while we are stating our ideas.

Even after I learned how to express my ideas effectively, when I spoke up, I was interrupted. When I lacked confidence in my ability to speak, I used to stop speaking as soon as someone would interrupt me. However, once I knew my ideas were creating value and I knew I was able to speak effectively, I was determined not to allow anyone to stop me.

How did I do that?

When someone interrupted me, I'd remain calm and raise my voice ever so slightly, ignore the interruption, and continue speaking. In most cases, the other person would stop. This was hard and awkward at times, but I was determined to command the respect I knew my ideas and I deserved. Staying calm in these moments is key, because the moment you get upset, your ability to communicate effectively diminishes.

I once had an experience with an individual who was just as persistent as I was. He kept speaking over me while I was expressing an idea that I really believed would create tremendous value for our organization. I looked him straight in the eye and said calmly, respectfully, and firmly, "Let me finish." I didn't tack on a "please" either. Why? Because he wasn't doing me a favor. I had the right to share my idea without being interrupted—an idea that would create value for our organization. Listening to me was in the best interest of everyone on the team—including him.

After the meeting, he came to apologize and thank me. He explained that he didn't intend to interrupt me and that he was working on his listening skills, so he appreciated the way I requested him to let me finish.

Over the next couple of months, this happened three or four times with different people in different meetings. I responded in the exact same way. It was difficult and awkward, but I knew I had to do it. Knowing that my ideas were creating value and needed to be heard gave me the confidence to stand firm in my belief that my ideas should be heard. Persistence and consistency are key.

> **INSIGHT**
>
> You teach others how to treat you based on what you will and won't accept.

My stubborn determination paid off. People stopped interrupting me—in meetings, on conference calls, even in watercooler and hallway conversations. In fact, my refusal to let others talk over me became part of my personal branding. People would joke: "Don't try to interrupt Shelmina; she won't let you." I took it as a compliment.

Biases Against You and Negative Stereotypes

Another barrier that can sabotage women's ability to contribute value at their maximum capacity is negative stereotypes and gender biases. If you are working in a male-dominated workplace, the reality is that because you're a woman, you'll deal with the gender biases (conscious and/or unconscious) and negative stereotypes that permeate workplace cultures today. Be aware of such biases and negative stereotypes so you can navigate them intentionally. People might question your capabilities; they might even question why you have a particular role or were given a particular assignment. Remember, their opinions don't have any power over you. Take every opportunity to educate them about your capabilities by contributing value at your maximum capacity. If you allow people to stop you from contributing value at your maximum capacity, you give your power to them. Not only do you and your organization miss out on your value contribution when this happens, but you also reinforce their biases and negative stereotypes.

Let me share a personal story to illustrate this important point.

Two years after moving into sales, I was assigned to a large, complex, and highly competitive must-win key deal. To craft a winning strategy, I needed some information from a man I'll call Bob. He was responsible for the overall relationship with this account.

Bob was blond, handsome, and accomplished and looked like most of his bosses and his team. One day I set up a meeting with him to get information that I needed. Instead of sharing the information I was asking for, he peppered me with the same question over and over: "Are you sure you can win this deal? This is going to be tough."

His behavior was a clear indication that he did not believe I was capable of winning this deal. This made me so uncomfortable that I cut the meeting short and left without all the information I needed. I was livid and went straight to my sales manager, Keith.

His office door was open, indicating he was available for walk-ins. (It would probably have been better for me if he'd been busy—I could've relaxed a bit and put my thoughts together.)

Keith invited me to take a seat, but his usual smile faded when he saw how upset I was. "What's going on?" he asked.

I launched into a tirade, "I just had a meeting with Bob, and I can't believe how

> **INSIGHT**
>
> When people question your capabilities, you can choose to let them get to you, or you can prove your capabilities and change their opinion.

he treated me. You should've seen the way he was talking to me! He clearly thinks I'm incapable of winning this deal. I'm not sure if I want to work with him."

"This is a must-win deal for us," Keith said calmly. "I assigned it to you because I know you can win it. You can't let his behavior stop you from winning this deal."

I protested: "He's questioning my capabilities. It infuriates me!"

"I've had a lot of people question my capabilities, and it used to infuriate me, too, but let me tell you—if I lost my cool every time someone did that, I wouldn't be here today."

Keith was also an underrepresented minority.

Since I knew Keith's coaching helped me tremendously in being successful in sales, I listened to him carefully.

He continued: "In this case, Bob is projecting his ignorance onto you. It's his problem, not yours. He's most likely never worked with anyone who looks like you and probably has biases and stereotypes that make him question your capabilities. By winning this deal, you can educate him and change his biases. Not only will he never question your capabilities again; he'll also change how he treats others who look like you. On the other hand, if you walk away from this deal, you'll reinforce his biases and stereotypes. It's a golden opportunity . . . ," and he smiled as he continued, "if you handle it right."

> **INSIGHT**
>
> When you notice negative stereotypes or gender biases, don't be intimidated. Instead, choose to show your worth by intentionally creating value at your maximum capacity.

Keith helped me rethink how I should approach Bob, and I was even more determined to win this deal. I was *not* going to let anyone get in my way. I set up another meeting with Bob, with the same intention of getting the information I needed to create a winning strategy. Bob's style hadn't changed, but I had. I went through my list of questions, and every time he peppered me with questions about my capabilities, I confidently said, "I need a few more questions answered. Once we're done with those, I'll be happy to answer whatever questions you have."

After I got the information I needed, I asked him what questions he had for me. As I answered his questions with confidence and competence, his style softened. And in the end, I won the deal.

You might have folks like Bob in your organization, but I also believe that the majority of men don't deliberately wake up in the morning with the intention of stopping women from contributing value. Instead, they may not have experienced the value that someone who looks like you or speaks like you can contribute. As more and more of us create value at our maximum capacity at every opportunity, the more others will have the opportunity to witness our capabilities and the value we create for our organizations, which will slowly but surely erode negative stereotypes and biases.

Here's the thing: You can't completely remove people's biases and negative stereotypes, but you can prevent their biases from impacting your performance and your ability to contribute value at your maximum capacity.

As a woman, and especially a woman of color, you'll encounter many biases and stereotypes in your career. Be prepared for it. Remember, you can't control people, but you can choose your response to their behavior. Think of their biases and negative stereotypes as background noise that you won't allow to distract you or break your confidence. See their behaviors as an opportunity to educate them so you can slowly but surely help dismantle negative stereotypes and gender biases—one person at a time.

Know deep down that the person you educated about your capabilities will not look at someone else who reminds them of you the same way. If we all take this upon ourselves, we will become change agents in dismantling negative biases and gender stereotypes. Everyone will eventually realize that women are capable of creating a tremendous amount of value.

Know When It's Time to Course-Correct

When you are creating value at your maximum capacity and it is not being recognized and rewarded by your organization, take your value elsewhere as my friend Sangeeta Singh-Kurtz did.

Sangeeta began her first postcollege journalism gig, an internship at a digital media company, when she was 23. Over the next two years, she made an unlivable wage in New York as she tried to find her footing in the journalism industry. It didn't take her long to realize she was one of the few people on staff who didn't come from a privileged background.

Sangeeta moved from the small city of Tacoma, Washington, the day after graduating college, with the sum of $700. Her internship, which paid minimum wage, lasted for three months, and she spent that time making herself indispensable to her managers. When her internship ended, she was hired as an editorial assistant, and her responsibilities tripled, but her pay barely changed. She worked evenings and weekends and lived paycheck to paycheck. It never occurred to her to ask for more money—she was just happy to be there.

Over time, Sangeeta had taken on responsibilities that were not a part of her job description, and when she asked to have them removed, her boss and HR representative smiled and told her how valuable she was. They shared they always envisioned her role to be "dynamic," and implied that if she wanted to stay at the company, she needed to stop complaining.

Three months after that discussion, she was given a promotion, largely thanks to the company's only nonwhite editor, who had taken her under his wing and suggested she replace another writer who'd been fired. She was ecstatic because she finally had the job she'd been working so hard for.

About a year into this role, an anonymous "salary transparency" document—noting factors such as race, gender, experience, title, etc.—began circulating around the office. This document revealed that she was making $30,000 less than the employee who was fired before her and tens of thousands less than colleagues in the same position and others who had the same or less credentials than she had. It was in that moment that she realized how severely underpaid she was, proving to her just how much the company really valued her. She started applying for jobs outside the company.

She spoke with an old colleague, a woman named Lily Kuo, the former Beijing bureau chief of the *Guardian* and now the China bureau chief of the *Washington Post*. Kuo advised her not to undersell herself when applying for new jobs. Sangeeta started shooting higher and landed interviews at companies she never thought she'd be capable of working at—and those same companies also offered her jobs. She accepted a higher position of senior editor with a better salary at *New York Magazine*. And most importantly, the company recognizes the value she contributes.

VALUE CREATION ACCELERATORS

Now that we have talked about headwinds, let's shift our attention to tailwinds which will help you accelerate your ability to create higher levels of value at your maximum capacity.

Soar with Your Competences

Your ability to create value is directly proportional to the competences you use in any given circumstance. Some of your competences create higher value for your organization than others.

Let me take a moment to differentiate among strengths, skills, and competence:

- A *strength* is defined by *The Britannica Dictionary* (online) as "the quality that allows someone to deal with problems in a determined and effective way." Your strengths are those things you're naturally good at. Think *curious, team player, enthusiastic, trustworthy, creative*, etc.
- A *skill* is something you can learn. Think *communication, time management, working collaboratively with a team*, etc.
- *Competence* is defined by the University of Nebraska–Lincoln's Human Resources Department as "the combination

of observable and measurable knowledge, skills, abilities and personal attributes that contribute to enhanced employee performance and ultimately result in organizational success." This combination enables you to perform something exceptionally well.

During my first job as a software engineer, I worked hard, contributed as much value as I could, and got rated well, but I was not earning big awards or being looked to as a role model. I was a good but not an exceptional software engineer. This position required a few of my competences, but not the ones that made me stand out. However, when I moved to systems engineering, my role was aligned with more of my competences that created higher levels of value for my clients and my organization. My value contribution soared, and so did my achievement. As a result, I created such high-level value that I crushed every expectation, both for my corporation and for my clients.

I received the highly coveted Rookie Systems Engineer of the Year award, which is how I wound up at that shiny mahogany table with Susan Whitney (mentioned earlier in Chapter 1).

Align yourself with roles in which you can soar with your competence.

Master Collaboration

Collaboration is the process of working together to create value with each other—this includes what we know, what we do, and how we think. When you collaborate, your ability to create value gets multiplied, because we can create more value combined than any one of us can individually: 1 + 1 becomes greater than 2.

Develop the skills needed for you to master collaboration including open-mindedness, intellectual curiosity, effective listening, effective communication, and cultural competence also share credit with and acknowledge the contributions of others and listen to the feelings and concerns of others.

When you collaborate effectively, you don't always need to have fully formed ideas. Instead, asking the right questions and being a part of a group that's open-minded will enable you to formulate answers through collaboration. Asking thought-provoking questions can result in a dialogue that will lead to tremendous value creation.

Collaboration is critical when you emerge as a leader. The higher you rise in a corporation, the more your success depends on your ability to collaborate with other stakeholders to create value for your organization. The sooner you master collaboration, the sooner you'll unlock your capability to create maximum value for yourself and your organization.

Lean into Your Authenticity and Uniqueness

Your authenticity and uniqueness are your super powers when it comes to creating unique and high value.

Going back to the earlier story at the beginning of this chapter, as I practiced overcoming my fears and speaking up effectively without allowing anyone to interrupt me, I started creating more value, which became my point of connection and collaboration with my team, my coworkers, and my boss.

I realized that my unique background and life journey enabled me to create unique value. Because I was unique and my life experiences were unique, my thought process was also unique. I saw and solved problems in a different way than did anyone else on my team. My differences, which I once thought were my weaknesses, were in reality my strengths, and I needed to recognize them as such. Once I leaned into my uniqueness, I created unique value that could neither be replaced nor replicated easily. Everyone started recognizing the value I was creating, and I started getting invitations to attend more meetings and join task forces. My company recognized my unique value, and that is why they extended my visa and sponsored me for my green card so I could live and work in the United States.

> **INSIGHT**
>
> When you lean into your authenticity, you create unique value.

You must lean into your uniqueness and authenticity by being true to yourself, and that includes your upbringing, life journey, values, character, and personality. Doing so allows you to bring forward your differentiated and unique value that only you can create. You'll become essential to the success of your organization, and your salary, power, and reputation will flourish as a result.

A STORY OF INTENTIONAL VALUE CREATION

Kathleen Hogan
Chief People Officer at Microsoft

As you and your career evolve and your circumstances change, you must be constantly vigilant about leaning into your uniqueness and your unique circumstances instead of trying to fit in and conceal a part of your authentic self. This is vividly illustrated by my friend and a woman whom I deeply respect and admire, Kathleen Hogan, chief people officer at Microsoft, who reports to CEO Satya Nadella. Here's her story, in her own words.

Before You Climb That Hill,
Make Sure There Isn't a Way Around It

"Covering" is a word that has taken on a relatively new meaning in the lexicon, but odds are, you've done it. We've all done it: Hidden a part of our authentic selves for deeply personal reasons—because we're afraid that others may think poorly of us, or may treat us differently, or may reject us.

The desire to fit in by hiding what makes us unique is human nature. We thrive on connection, and commonality is often the basis of connection. Author and vulnerability researcher Brené Brown says this: "Fitting in is about assessing a situation and becoming who you need to be to be accepted."

I'll tell you a secret I learned the hard way: It's so much more difficult to cover—to fit in—than to bring your real, authentic self to a situation. Acceptance is a steep tax on a life lived in hiding.

Uncovering Covering

In 2007, I was diagnosed with breast cancer. As you may imagine, this diagnosis rocked my world. I had a young son who needed me, and I was actively growing my career at Microsoft, leading the global services organization.

My first instinct was to hide this news from all but those who absolutely needed to know.

I told my family and direct reports, and that was it. I rationalized this decision as wanting to keep some semblance of normality—to maintain my image as "Kathleen," not "Kathleen-who's-fighting-cancer." I could hear the hallway whispers and see the sympathy cards before they existed—and told myself I didn't want that.

In keeping with the image that everything was fine—I was fine—I took the proactive step of having a wig made of my own hair. A preemptive strike before my hair fell out. "How clever I am," I thought.

Fast-forward to a big event for the Customer Service and Support organization, in which I was introducing our CEO at the time, Steve Ballmer. I was in the midst of chemotherapy and had lost my hair.

Enter the wig.

I had a decision to make as I was getting ready the morning of the event: Adhere the wig with tape, which is more secure but itchy. Or put on the wig and use a headband, which is more comfortable but not as secure.

I opted for comfort.

The buildup for Steve's entrance was energetic, to say the least. We had a group of folks on stage beating drums, and the audience had drums as well. The entire room was bouncing with a fever pitch of excitement to see and hear Steve B— as we called him—in person.

And all I could think about was my hair.

Steve came onstage in this rowdy way that's uniquely his, and he started drumming on my shoulders. I was so worried he was going to accidentally tug on my hair, the wig would fall off, and I'd be outed in front of my entire organization.

I can laugh about this now, but in the moment, what should have been pure joy was just plain terror. I can still feel how exhausted I was, fussing daily with my wig, my eyebrows, my eyelashes. I was fighting for my life and worried about my appearance. Worried about what people would think.

A Do-Over

It's not often in life we get do-overs on pivotal moments, but for some reason, I did. I certainly didn't ask for this mulligan, but my body and cancer decided I was going to have it.

In 2018, I was diagnosed with breast cancer, again. And once again, it coincided with a large event. This time I was keynoting our Global HR Conference, the biannual event for the HR organization I now led at Microsoft.

Once the shock of the diagnosis wore off, I again had a decision to make. I could walk on stage and share with my work family what was going on in my life. Or I could cover by not acknowledging it and pretend everything was fine.

This time I made the decision to tell my story onstage.

And something incredible happened. As I stood on stage in front of 2,000 HR professionals at Microsoft and told them I had cancer, I felt the tension in my shoulders melt away. Watching them react with hands over mouths and tears in their eyes, I could breathe. When they clapped for me—well, I had tears of my own.

I'm happy to report that I'm once again cancer-free. And the support I received from my team lifted my spirits day in and day out as I fought through my treatments.

What I've Learned

The first time I was diagnosed with cancer, I scripted and overengineered my outward image. Worried I'd be judged, deemed weak, or rejected, I hid. And hiding was exhausting. The second time, I let people in. I stood under a (literal) spotlight and admitted I was scared, distracted, and fighting. I hoped sharing my struggle might help others who were fighting a secret battle.

I feel lucky to be able to tell my story in the hopes that others may relate. When you attempt to predict how people are going to react to you being you, you undermine their credibility. When you curate an image that you think people expect, you steal their opportunity to see you in your full light. *The lesson:* Don't stop shining, because you'll leave people in the dark about who you truly are—and that's not fair to you or them.

My hope is that we ultimately get to a place in the world where "covering" as a term is retired because we don't need it anymore. Until then, next time you're tempted to hide, ask yourself if the benefit is worth the cost.

INTENTIONAL EXERCISES

Now it's time to create and execute your strategy of Intentional Value Creation so you can create maximum value in all your interactions.

As you become intentional about creating value, you will stop being on autopilot, and you'll create more value in every hour of every day than you ever did before.

Let's start with the Introspection section so you can gain knowledge of where you currently stand in terms of value creation; then we'll move to the Application section to apply the insights you learned in this chapter so you can intentionally start increasing the value you create in all interactions, and we'll wrap things up with Reflection and Celebration to look back, course-correct, and celebrate your successes of applying this strategy until you master it. Let's get started.

Introspection

Let's start by your answering some questions to help you understand your current state of value creation. Ask yourself:

Understand Value Creation

- How is value measured in my role?
- How is value measured in my organization?
- Do I take pride in the value I create for my organization?
- What are my top contributions to increasing value for my boss and my organization?
- Do I currently contribute value less than, equal to, or exceeding my boss's expectations?
- Can I think of a time when I had to pick between two priorities and chose the one that I received first or seemed the most urgent even though it created less value?
- On a scale of 1 to 10, with 10 being the best, how would I rate myself in terms of the value I create in all my interactions?

Internal Barriers and Self-Limiting Beliefs

- What internal barriers and self-limiting beliefs are stopping me from contributing value at my maximum capacity?
- Why do I have those beliefs?
- Am I deeply aware that I can change my beliefs?
- Have I ever tried changing my beliefs? What was the result?
- If I became the author of my program, what would I change so I could contribute value at my maximum capacity?
- Have I ever managed the voices in my head?
- Do I experience workplace fears? Which ones?
- How do I deal with those fears?

External Barriers

- Do any of my "unders" keep me from contributing value? For example, underrepresented, undereducated, or underexperienced?
- Do people openly question my capabilities?
- What other external barriers are stopping me from contributing value at my maximum capacity?
- How do I respond to biases and negative stereotypes?
- Is there a time when someone else's behavior stopped me from contributing maximum value?

Communication Skills

- On a scale of 1 to 10, with 10 being the best, how would I rate my communication skills?
- Am I afraid of speaking up in meetings?
- What could I achieve if I faced that fear?
- Does anyone interrupt me when I'm speaking? If so, how do I respond to those interruptions?
- Do people listen when I speak? If not, why not?
- Do my ideas get heard and implemented? If not, why not?
- On a scale of 1 to 10, with 10 being intentionally powerful words, how do I rate my choice of words when communicating at work?

Collaboration Skills

- On a scale of 1 to 10, with 10 being the best, how would I rate my collaboration skills?
- Do I display my intellectual curiosity by asking thought-provoking questions—that in turn lead to tremendous value creation?
- Do I invite collaboration by listening effectively with an open mind?

- Do I acknowledge and praise my colleagues?
- Am I sensitive to different work styles and cultural dynamics?

Soar with Competence

- What are my core competences? As a reminder, this should include strengths such as curiosity, enthusiasm, empathy, and energy; skills such as time management, communication, collaboration, and organization; acquired knowledge such as data analytics, computer programming, accounting, or marketing; and personal attributes such as trustworthiness, integrity, and grit. (Save this list as we'll be referring to it in other chapters).
- Have I internalized my competence?
- Am I using my competences to create high levels of value in my current role? If the answer is no, what role would use my competences that will create higher levels of value?
- Do I enjoy my job?
- Do people seek me out for my competences?
- Does my job energize me?

Lean into Uniqueness and Authenticity

- Am I using my unique competences to create unique value?
- Am I true to myself? This includes my upbringing, journey, values, character, and personality.
- Do I view my differences as my strengths or weaknesses?
- What are the aspects of myself that I am tempted to "cover"?
- How do the ways I try to fit in limit my ability to contribute my unique value?
- How can my unique perspective help me contribute unique value?
- Do I feel that my value is so special that I can't be easily replaced?

Application

Now that you know where you currently stand in terms of creating value, let's work to ensure you apply the insights you learned in this chapter so you can move from your current state of value creation to your desire state of intentionally contributing value at your maximum capacity in all your interactions.

Let's get started by adding "Intentional Value Creation" to your priorities in your PSP. This will serve as a weekly reminder to intentionally create value in all your interactions. This reminder will also ensure you are not on autopilot reacting to whatever comes your way.

How can you create maximum value in all your interactions?

First and foremost, begin your workday by setting an intention of creating value at your maximum capacity in all your interactions. This will ensure that you move from your current state of value creation to your desire state. Here are a few ideas that will help you:

- If you have any internal barriers, dismantle them by trying different approaches, such as changing your self-limiting beliefs, managing the voices in your head, exercising your PQ to choose an empowering response, or becoming the author of your program and expunging your self-limiting beliefs.
- If you have any external barriers, dismantle them by focusing all your attention on creating value at your maximum capacity in all your interactions. Naysayers with biases and negative stereotypes can say or do what they want, but the reality is that if you don't react to what these people say, they have no power over you. Don't allow their behavior to drive you; instead, educate them by creating value at your maximum capacity.
- Internalize your competence. If you need help, read the list you created of your competence in Chapter 1, the last thing before you go to bed and first thing every morning until you

114

know how competent you are—in every core of your being. This helps you stay your course when someone undermines your capabilities.

- Improve your communication skills.
- Master collaboration skills to create a multiplier effect.
- Soar with your competence to create higher levels of value.
- Be proud of and lean into your authentic self to create unique value.
- Whatever else you need to do.

As you start executing on your strategy of Intentional Value Creation, you'll improve your ability to create value. Every single day you'll intentionally create value, which will get compounded over time and result in your surpassing every expectation you set for yourself and others set for you, while also moving you faster toward your definitions of success. You will get known for and noticed for the value you are creating.

Reflection and Celebration

During your weekly reflection time, ask yourself the following questions:

- What value did I create for my own success this week?
- What value did I create for the success of my boss this week?
- What value did I contribute to the success of my organization this week?
- Did I contribute value at my maximum capacity in all my interactions?

If the answer to the fourth question is no, course-correct without beating yourself up. You can't belittle yourself to greatness. It's important to focus on progress and not on perfection. If you need a reminder, put a calendar reminder to intentionally create value at your maximum capacity every few hours to ensure you don't fall back to autopilot.

No matter what, congratulate yourself for the answers you wrote down for the first three questions, because that's value you *did* create. Reflect upon those answers, be grateful for the opportunity, and celebrate yourself for being of value to your boss and to your organization. This process will motivate you to create more value the following week. And over time, you will master this strategy and Intentional Value Creation will become a habit.

Take pride in the value you create. As the opening quote by Oprah Winfrey states, "When you undervalue what you do, the world will undervalue who you are."

SET YOUR INTENTIONS

Promise yourself:

- I will change my self-limiting beliefs and exercise my Power Quotient to dismantle any internal and external barriers that limit my ability to create value.
- I will intentionally focus on creating value at my maximum capacity in all my interactions.
- I will contribute value for the sake of my own success as well as the success of my boss and my entire organization.

5

INTENTIONAL GROWTH

*I learned to always take on things I'd never
done before. Growth and comfort do not coexist.*

GINNI ROMETTY,
former IBM CEO and chair

THE FIFTH strategy that will help you show your worth and emerge
as a leader is Intentional Growth. When you show up to work every
day with the intention of growing at your maximum capacity, your
daily incremental growth will get compounded over time and become
transformational. The only guarantee that you will be better tomorrow
is if you experience growth today. The more you grow, the higher the
value you create for everyone you interact with and your organization.
Your growth will be reflected in your performance and will move you
faster toward achieving both your short-term and long-term visions
of success.

Regardless of how much value you create in your current role, if
you don't intentionally seek and seize opportunities for growth, you'll

continue to create value at your current level, which will limit your ability to emerge as a leader.

Every interaction or experience provides you with two opportunities: what you give and what you get. What you give is the value that you create, and what you get is the value that interaction or experience creates for you, which translates into your growth.

When I reflect upon who I was when I started my career at 25 and compare it with who I am now, I'm in awe of the growth I've experienced, in terms of both personal development and professional development. My 25-year-old self could never have imagined in her wildest dreams that she'd grow into the leader I've become—one who went from being afraid to speak up in meetings to a woman who speaks on stages to thousands of women globally. And one who would become a senior executive in a large technology company. All this was made possible because of my growth. While there were many contributing factors to my growth, stepping outside my comfort zone helped me the most.

In Chapter 3, on work-life balance, I shared with you that after I emerged from my personal crisis and found a good work-life balance, the personal growth I experienced set me up for accelerated success in my career. In just over two years, I'd achieved my professional goal of my five-year definition of success, which was to get promoted to a second line sales leader. This position meant I had the opportunity to lead a team of 7 sales leaders and 150 salespeople with a target of generating $950 million in revenue annually. That was my first role as a leader of leaders, and I had much to learn. As I learned advanced leadership skills, I started to thrive in that role and achieved my short-term definition of success.

This success inspired me to aim even higher. I redefined my professional goal of my long-term definitions of success: *Become an IBM executive.* This was not a dream I was even capable of dreaming when I started my career, and the word "executive" was not even in my vocabulary when I was growing up.

As is the case at many organizations, competition was extremely fierce for executive positions at IBM. The positions are scarce, the openings are infrequent, and the competition is among the best of the best candidates from inside and outside the organization.

I set up some time with Susan Whitney to ask for her guidance on how I could get a chance to compete for executive roles. At this time, she was a senior executive in our hardware business, a business in which I had a track record of success for over 10 years. I was hoping she'd sponsor me for an executive role in our hardware business, but instead, she gave me the following guidance: "If you want to get promoted to an IBM executive, you should consider moving into our software or services businesses." She explained that IBM was investing in those businesses as they were expanding, and that's where the executive openings would be. She continued, "Also, you'll learn some highly relevant and marketable skills in these areas of expansion, not just for IBM but for our industry."

INSIGHT

As you grow, new possibilities will open up for you to rise higher.

Even though I knew very little about our software or services business, I decided to take a chance on myself and apply for those jobs, as I now knew they would set me up to compete for executive positions. I did some research and learned that our services business was the fastest-growing business at IBM, so I decided to try to find a role in it. At IBM, moving from the hardware business to our services business was like applying for a new job in a new company, and I knew I needed to find someone who would make introductions. So I reached out to an executive in our services organization, Carolyn Maher, whom I'd known from past interactions.

Carolyn was the most senior-level services executive in Seattle, and we had a great experience working together previously. During those times, I gained great admiration for her leadership skills, and I'd learned a lot from her. She was also impressed with how I navigated challenges, and we built a good relationship as a result. I knew she was highly successful and respected within our services organization.

Carolyn shared that our services business was looking for strong sales leaders and that she'd be happy to introduce me to other executives in the services organization who had openings for a sales leadership position at my level. Her introduction carried her credibility with it.

INSIGHT

Always know your industry trends, where your company is investing, and what skills will make you more relevant and marketable.

A few weeks later, I interviewed and accepted a position in one of the fastest-growing businesses within our services organization. Their performance was suffering, and employee morale was very low. They needed a strong sales leader to turn things around, and I was ready to take on a role that would increase my chances of getting promoted to an IBM executive—or so I thought.

Two days after I started my role, I joined my first conference call where my team discussed our largest deals for the quarter; I couldn't understand 75 percent of the conversations thanks to the notorious use of acronyms in the tech industry. This made me feel extremely uncomfortable. In my last two leadership roles, I was familiar with the business I was leading, and over time I'd become an expert and understood the business thoroughly. Now I was supposed to be leading this business, and I didn't even understand what people were talking about! I was pushed completely outside my comfort zone and found myself wondering, "How can I possibly add any value, and how can I possibly lead this organization, let alone be successful in turning it around?"

On top of this, I learned that one of the gentlemen reporting to me had been the leading candidate before I was interviewed, and there were others on my new team who believed I got this job because I was a woman of color. All of this made me miss my old team and my old job, and I found myself starting to panic. My mental chatter went wild with my self-doubting thoughts: "What part of me was stupid enough to take this job? This is a terrible mistake. I'm doomed to fail in this role. Becoming an IBM executive isn't in the cards for me."

Fortunately, by that point in my career, I'd improved my ability to exercise my PQ and was able to shift my thoughts fairly quickly to "How lucky I am to have a role in a fast-growing business, which could increase my chances of becoming an IBM executive. I was pushed completely outside my comfort zone when I first moved into sales and when I was going through my personal crisis. If I could figure out how to navigate my discomfort and challenges then, I can do it again now."

However, I knew that I needed more than just a shift in my mindset. I also needed to get some help. So I decided to speak to a mentor who had successfully made a transition from our hardware business to our services business herself. She gave me some great advice. She shared: "It's natural to be uncomfortable in a new role, especially in a business you know nothing about. It shows you're pushing your boundaries— that's how you grow. You're not expected to know everything about a business when you start. Just listen and learn. Be patient with yourself. Once you learn the business, only *then* can you contribute value with your sales leadership expertise—which is why they hired you."

After speaking to her, I changed my approach. Instead of impa- tiently wanting to contribute value, I went to work every day with the intention of listening, learning, and growing my knowledge of the busi- ness while also being deeply aware of the fact that I was a highly com- petent sales leader who'd be able to contribute value once I understood the business and the challenges that were hindering our performance.

Many of us have a desire to prove ourselves by contributing value right away. In most cases, this serves us well, but when we're in uncharted territories, we must give ourselves enough time to listen and learn before we can contribute value. Be patient with yourself, and if needed, ask for help from those who have successfully navigated a similar situation.

Many women also have a tendency to spend too much time and energy focusing on what we don't know or can't do. Instead, balance your thoughts by also focusing on what you do know and what you can bring to the table. That balance is key.

I knew I had a lot to learn, but I had underestimated just how much. Fortunately, my inherent intellectual curiosity became a critical growth driver. Every hour of every day, I intentionally sought opportunities to learn and grow. I learned from my boss, my peers, my mentors, my team, our clients, and even our competitors. I became a sponge, soaking up all the knowledge I could. As I learned about our business, challenges, and clients and especially how they made buying decisions, I slowly but surely started contributing value. My team's expertise combined with my sales and sales leadership expertise resulted in some impressive wins, but unfortunately it was too late for us to meet our quarterly revenue and profit targets.

INSIGHT

When you don't meet a desired outcome after you give it your best shot, reframe your measure of success to the growth you experienced.

Before this, I'd never missed my quarterly targets, so I felt like a failure. I hated that I missed my business objective and thought I'd lost my chance of becoming an IBM executive. But once again, thanks to my PQ, I quickly got out of my funk and shifted my thinking again. Instead of seeing this quarter as a failure, I thought about just how much I had grown. I recognized that I'd learned how to lead a new team and a new business I knew nothing about. I also recognized that I'd learned how to earn the support of my sales leader who didn't get my job and deal with people who had doubted my capabilities, thinking I was given the job because I was a woman of color.

I had used every challenge as an opportunity to learn and grow. I let my behavior and expertise speak for themselves. Not once did I react to anyone's behavior nor treat people any differently even though

I could clearly see they were doubting my capabilities. I kept my power at all times by carefully choosing my responses and conducting myself as a leader who wouldn't let naysayers impact her performance. I was able to do this more easily by now because I'd been through that situation many times before that—mostly as an individual contributor. This time I was being doubted by the people who worked for me—that hadn't happened before. Regardless of who doubts your capabilities, if you let that impact your performance negatively, you're giving them power over you. You must never give your power to anyone. It's yours to own at all times.

Rather than mourning the fact that I'd missed my quarterly revenue and profit targets, I used my PQ to shift my thoughts to how much I had learned and grown during the quarter. I reframed my definition of success from meeting my quarterly target to appreciating the incredible growth I had experienced. This energized me to move forward with everything I'd learned.

My growth set me up for accelerated success in the following quarter. We started winning some impressive and highly competitive deals. I celebrated the people who won those deals, and I encouraged an environment of learning and growing. I instituted "learning reviews" for every deal—win or lose—so we could continue to learn and grow from every experience.

We kept refining our strategy, and as we learned more, we won more deals and achieved our second-quarter revenue and profit targets. The team was energized as never before, and the morale of the team members significantly improved. By the end of the year, we finished so strong that not only did we make up the shortfall of the first quarter, but we also surpassed our yearly revenue and profit targets. We became one of the top-performing teams. Our clients gave us rave reviews. On top of that, I exceeded every single business objective for the year, which included revenue targets, profit targets, employee morale, and client satisfaction. The fact that we hadn't made our first-quarter targets didn't even matter in the long run. My team and I received multiple recognitions for our year-end results.

When I paused to reflect upon that year, I realized just how much I'd learned and grown in my role. The daily incremental growth had turned into transformational growth. Achieving success in this role grew my confidence exponentially. Had I not pushed myself completely outside my comfort zone, I'd have never known I was capable of achieving success in a business I knew nothing about and team I had never worked with before.

At the end of the year, I was invited for a one-year growth assignment to job-shadow Rodney Adkins as his executive assistant. Upon completion of that assignment, I received multiple offers for executive positions in our services and software businesses. My experience of turning around an underperforming services business I knew nothing about and winning over the team that doubted my capabilities gave the decision makers and me the confidence that I could successfully lead any business. And I continued to do just that. I kept taking positions that pushed me further and further outside my comfort zone, which created a platform for me to create an upward spiral for growing my competence and confidence. This propelled me to become a senior executive and one of the highest-ranking women of color at IBM.

> **INSIGHT**
>
> The most important benefit of stepping outside your comfort zone is uncovering new capabilities you did not even know you had.

I've continued to push myself outside my comfort zone today, even as I write this book. Writing isn't my core competence, and this book has been very challenging for me. I'm still learning and growing every step of the way. But what keeps me going is my "why" of writing this book—to help you emerge as a leader.

STEP OUTSIDE YOUR COMFORT ZONE

As the opening quote of this chapter states, "Growth and comfort do not coexist." Stepping outside your comfort zone will be your key growth driver. In order for you to emerge as a leader, thrive once you become one, and keep rising higher, it is imperative that you consistently step outside your comfort zone, navigate discomfort, and grow as a result of that experience. Intentionally seek opportunities that will push you outside your comfort zone now,

> **INSIGHT**
>
> Setbacks from which you learn and grow aren't failures. They're part of your growth.

not only so you can discover just how capable you are, but also so you remember that you've been pushed outside your comfort zone before and can do it again. In this process you will also learn what your limitations are, and that knowledge is equally important to make better decisions in the future. The more you practice navigating discomfort, the more confidence you'll gain in your ability to enter uncharted waters.

The following four steps will help you step outside your comfort zone:

1. **Remember that you're not the voices in your head.** Whenever you even think of stepping outside your comfort zone, you'll inevitably hear your voice of fear saying, "What if I fail?" This is normal, especially when you first get started. As you learned in Chapter 4, exercise your PQ and engage your voice of courage. Intentionally shift your thoughts to "What if I don't fail?," "What can I learn from this experience?," or "How can I grow from this experience?" Remember that you aren't the voices in your head. Instead, you're the one who hears them, and you can use your PQ to scan your mental chatter and choose a response that will fuel growth.

2. **Ask for help when you need it.** Know that if you struggle, you can seek help from your boss, mentors, trusted advisors, and

colleagues. Successful people have been in your shoes before, so they'll relate to your struggles and be willing to help. An added bonus of this is that as they watch you struggle and grow, you'll earn their admiration and respect. They can even become your future sponsor, which we'll talk about in Chapter 6, "Intentional Relationships."

3. **Own the narrative of your experience.** Every time you wonder if you made the right decision to step outside your comfort zone, think back to other uncomfortable experiences you've navigated in your life or career and change your narrative to "If I could navigate that, I can and will learn and grow from this." Create a narrative of growth that will keep you moving forward stronger.

4. **Congratulate yourself or reframe failure.** If you achieve your desired outcome when you push yourself out of your comfort zone, congratulate and celebrate yourself. Pause and reflect upon your growth, and seek another role or opportunity that will push you even further outside your comfort zone.

   If you don't achieve your desired outcome, don't consider yourself a failure. Instead, reflect upon the growth this experience provided and call that success, knowing that your growth will accelerate your future success.

   How you view setbacks is key to continued success. If you consider yourself a failure, you won't be energized to keep pursuing more success. You haven't failed until you decide you have and you give up. Always remember that there's no such thing as failure; instead, the most important thing is what you've learned and how much you've grown so you can be better prepared for future success. Don't take temporary failures to heart and beat yourself up. While those setbacks may seem big in the moment, they're really just part of your long-term growth trajectory.

Remember, your long-term success isn't determined by one experience. Instead, it's about staying in the game, learning, growing, and playing for the long term.

What may seem like a failure is the perfect platform for growth. In fact, I believe it's necessary to experience setbacks so you know that you are stretching yourself and you will also know you can bounce back. Setbacks build resilience, and that resilience is a pathway to growth.

We women are often too harsh on ourselves and we take setbacks very personally and in turn view ourselves as failures. We don't like to disappoint ourselves or anyone else. There is a difference between failing and thinking of yourself as a failure. I can't count the number of times I've had women tell me: "I'm such a loser! I'm a failure!" This thinking depletes us of our ambition and energy. It creates a downward spiral and can stop us from future success if we're not careful.

> **INSIGHT**
>
> The only time you actually fail is when you give up.

The reality is that your individual outcomes aren't what matter most over time; instead, it's your growth, which becomes the starting point for your next experience and stays with you forever.

OTHER TOOLS TO ACCELERATE YOUR GROWTH

In addition to pushing yourself outside your comfort zone, there are other ways that will enable you to intentionally grow at your maximum capacity. Let's discuss some.

Move to High-Growth Sectors

In order to accelerate your growth, seek roles in organizations that are experiencing growth. Such environments will provide more opportunities for you to grow. Don't get stuck in jobs with no room for growth.

One of my mentees, Chinara Satkeeva, who is currently a senior technology manager at Google, did just that. Upon graduation in 2009 from the University of Montana with a degree in political science, she accepted a role at JPMorgan Chase working as a bank teller. In the middle of the financial crisis, she was just happy to have a job! She was highly valued by her boss and received several promotions. However, she didn't see opportunities for further growth, so she started looking elsewhere in 2015.

She didn't know much about technology, but she saw the growth in that sector and knew she could translate her financial services capabilities into value for Google. She used her network and found her first job as a product specialist for a financial comparison product. At the time, this was a part-time job and paid less money than her current job, but she took it because she knew it would provide her opportunities for growth. She has successfully transitioned to an entirely different type of work and, as she had expected, has experienced tremendous growth. Today, she advises students and professionals looking to transition careers just as she did.

Seek and Apply Feedback

Another way to experience growth is to seek and apply feedback. When I look back at my career journey, I can see plainly that if I didn't have people who cared enough about me to provide feedback for improvement, I wouldn't have grown the way I did, and I certainly wouldn't have become the leader I am today. Receiving feedback from my bosses, mentors, colleagues, and team was instrumental for my growth. It also made me aware of blind spots that otherwise could've easily reduced my chances of success.

Let me share a personal story about feedback.

When I received my first promotion to sales leader, IBM used a 360-degree performance review tool, in which I received feedback from my boss as well as my team. Multiple members of my team said something along the lines of "I love the fact that Shelmina is a straight shooter. She's truly vested in my success—however, sometimes when she provides feedback for improvement, she's honest to a point that it hurts." Others simply said, "She's brutally honest."

I was shocked. My intention was to help them, not hurt them! Obviously, my current approach wasn't working, and their feedback made me aware of a very important blind spot. Their feedback was necessary for me to recognize my errors, and as a result, I got training so I could provide feedback more effectively.

I learned how to provide feedback and changed my branding from someone who was brutally honest while providing feedback to someone who did so in a kind and firm way.

In April 2016, I'd invited Kathleen Hogan, the chief people officer at Microsoft (remember her story from Chapter 4), to give a keynote at Young Women Empowered, an organization whose board I served on. She spoke about the importance of seeking feedback for professional development regardless of how high you are in an organization. The higher you rise in an organization, the harder feedback becomes to obtain. In Kathleen's case, she reported directly to CEO Satya Nadella, so there was only one person higher than her. However, she knows feedback is just as critical for an executive as it is at any other stage—maybe even more so, because the higher you climb, the more people you impact.

She shared this advice: "If you start by asking for areas of improvement, people may not be comfortable sharing their thoughts right away, especially if you're at a higher level than they are. Instead, start out by asking for two areas they believe you excel at. This will be easy for them. Once they start speaking, engage in a dialogue and then ask for two areas where you can improve. That seems to do the trick. Find people who will tell you what you need to hear in order to improve— that's the only way you can improve."

And when it comes to receiving feedback, practice asking sincerely and receiving gratefully. No matter the delivery, accept feedback as a gift for growth because that's exactly what it is.

Commit to Lifelong Learning

Seek opportunities to learn and grow in order to prepare yourself for your long-term definition of success. Today, there are a remarkable number of content platforms that you can learn from, including formal education, books, podcasts, TED Talks, experiences, conferences, online courses, reading content by people you respect and admire, and more.

In addition to learning from your day-to-day experiences which includes observing people, there are other ways you can learn. It's important that you know how you learn best. Is it by reading, listening, watching, or doing things?

Whatever way you choose to learn, it's also important that you're intentional about why, what, how, and when you're learning. It is not about learning for the sake of learning; it is about intentionally learning skills which will move you faster toward your visions of success. For example, if the role you want in five years will require you to manage the profit and loss of a project, take online classes or register for a course in finance to prepare yourself for it.

One important point to make is that it's crucial you actually apply what you learn so you are intentionally growing. If you're not careful, you could get caught in the loop of constantly learning but never applying those learnings and knowledge. It's better to read one book and apply the knowledge you gained than to read five books just for the sake of reading.

Keep in mind that learning is typically not an urgent task on your to-do list, so it's easy to deprioritize it. Be aware of this, and don't let your learning fall through the cracks. Prioritize and make time for it.

A STORY OF INTENTIONAL GROWTH

Melissa Kilby
Executive Director of Girl Up

Girl Up is a United Nations Foundation initiative "by girls, for girls." I've had the honor of serving on the advisory board for the past five years and have personally witnessed Melissa's growth during that time. Here's her story of how feedback made her the leader she is today.

"Your leadership style is hurting people." I received this feedback early on as a manager and leader.

Today, one of my leadership superpowers is how I give and receive feedback. My other strength at work is my ability to "get sh*t done," though that strength was almost my undoing, too. It made me an incredibly valuable team member and allowed me to take a few quick steps up the chain early in my career. But that focus and work style didn't serve me well as a manager or on my way to becoming a leader. And even to this day, I have to keep those urges at bay and in check. I've come a long way.

Candidly, I've always seen myself as a leader. I think I was born with an innate desire to be in charge, of knowing a better way to do something, and of honestly, really enjoying telling other people what to do—which I can own now. As I look back at Melissa in school, I never really got to flex that leadership desire because I wasn't really showing up to actually lead, I just wanted to be named "leader" of this club or that club. I was never selected by my peers for these roles though, and that hurt because I didn't understand it. Seeing yourself as a leader and wanting to be a leader don't actually equal leading. As a teenager, this was all very confusing to me. I knew that I could lead, that I had the ability to manage and delegate, that I was smart and passionate, and that I had good ideas. As I look back now, 20 years later, I see clearly that I was missing the part of leadership that's the most important: serving others, leading people toward a better outcome for a broader community for the good of others, not for our own ambition. I thought of leadership as a noun, a title, a destination. What I know now is that leadership functions as both a verb—"to lead"—and a noun, since it's also a journey, one filled with lessons and learning. I've found the harder the lesson, the more important to your growth. The worse it makes you feel, the more important it is to listen, open yourself to it, and absorb it.

As I entered my career and found a job and a path that I loved, my ambition had an outlet that allowed for that ability to show up, execute, get things done, be 100 percent reliable, and be valued and celebrated—all of which set me up for my first management experience. I raised my hand for everything, and I applied for all the internal opportunities—even when I wasn't qualified. I impressed my managers and my leaders, and I made myself invaluable to them. This wasn't an election; this was a place I could earn my way to the next step. I fast-tracked this process and could finally see my path to leadership. In my mind, if I wasn't trying to win a popularity contest, all I had to do was keep impressing my boss and I'd keep moving forward and up.

That worked until it didn't, until it wasn't enough. I still needed to learn, to internalize and embrace that to be a good manager and a good leader, it couldn't be about me and my ambition all the time, or even most or some of the time. I got

132

some really hard feedback a few years into my management journey, feedback that rocked my core. My boss and collaborator shared with me that my almost militant "get sh*t done" style was incredibly challenging for my team. My ambition "to be a leader" wasn't taking into account what my team actually needed from me. And I was also hurting people, which was absolutely not my intention. My boss gave me this feedback to help me see myself through the eyes of my team, giving me a chance to match my intention to my impact. I was pretty devastated. I sat with that feedback and reflected on it for a long time and just let it hurt until I felt the change within. I still think back to that experience when I get stressed and feel myself shift back into execution mode or realize I've taken my eyes off the real goal of serving others.

As I processed the feedback I was receiving, I realized this wasn't the manager or the leader that I wanted to be, and something shifted in that moment. I truly understood that my team and other people—and how I made them feel and how they felt about me—were more important than accomplishing any one task or project. I always cared, but the reality was that this wasn't evident in my actual interactions. Up until this point, my boss was happy because I was 100 percent reliable to get the job done. She never had to worry about anything I oversaw. We had a lot of good conversations about how in being so hyperfocused on delivering results, I was missing the most important element.

Getting that feedback, and not being defensive or turning away from it, actually taking it in and feeling all the feelings, was a transformational moment for me. Without that moment and my response to it, I don't believe I'd be where I am today.

That specific feedback alone was enough of a game changer, but the perspective, valuation, and response I experienced by getting and giving feedback created an even bigger shift for me—and that specific moment started me on my current leadership journey. I was so grateful for the feedback. I was grateful to have the opportunity to change and do better. I still hold onto that feeling and the important realization that feedback is a gift.

As I've progressed through my career and as I began my role with Girl Up 10 years ago, I brought that spirit with me. I came in as a different kind of manager and with the goal of becoming a real leader. I started from a place of listening and serving. I've worked to keep that at the center of my style and approach ever since. I crave and relish all feedback, the good, the bad, and the ugly. I receive those gifts with open arms. And trust me, sometimes it's still really hard to hear the bad. But I sit with it, absorb it, understand it, and dissect it—and it always makes me better.

One of the things I'm most proud of is how I've transitioned my appreciation in receiving feedback to my approach to how I give it. Because I've received hard feedback—before that transformational moment, in that moment, and since that moment—I've been able to transfer that to my approach in giving hard constructive feedback. It's an approach based on two vital "hows": how I can serve and lead and coach and partner in those moments and how I can center empathy in my management and empathy in my expectations. I've been the subject of those hard conversations. I'll never forget how that feels.

Feedback is a gift. Listening is the point.

INTENTIONAL EXERCISES

Now it's time to create and execute your strategy of Intentional Growth. Let's start with Introspection, so you can gain knowledge of your current growth trajectory. Then we'll move to the Application section, so you can apply the insights you learned in this chapter and intentionally start seeking growth in all your interactions and grow at your maximum capacity. We'll wrap things up with Reflection and Celebration to look back, course-correct, and celebrate your successes of applying this strategy until you master it. Let's get started.

Introspection

Take the time to think through your answers to the following questions to gain knowledge of your current growth trajectory.

Step Outside My Comfort Zone
- When was the last time I took on a project or applied for a position for which I didn't feel qualified?
- How did I grow from it?
- How do I navigate discomfort?
- How often do I seek help?
- Does fear of failure keep me from stepping outside my comfort zone?
- Do I recognize the power of my narrative?
- Which positions can I take that will provide transformational growth opportunities to assist me in acquiring competences that will move me toward my long-term vision of success?
- How do I view setbacks?

Move to High-Growth Sectors

- Am I experiencing growth in my current role?
- What relevant and marketable competences am I learning?
- On a scale of 1 to 10, with 10 being the best, how would I rate myself in terms of the growth I experience in all my interactions?
- Does my current position provide growth that will prepare me for my long-term definitions of success?
- Does my current organization have positions that are aligned with my long-term definitions of success?
- Is my sector growing?

Seek and Apply Feedback

- Whom do I receive feedback from?
- How do I currently receive feedback?
- How often do I receive feedback?
- Should I be seeking additional or more frequent feedback?
- Should I be seeking feedback from other people? If so, who?
- What specific feedback has helped me grow?

Commit to Lifelong Learning

- What are some specific things I've learned from my day-to-day challenges?
- What other ways do I learn?
- Who do I learn from?
- How do I learn best?
- When I do learn, do I apply my learning?
- Does my company offer learning for skills I need?
- What additional business skills and knowledge would help me achieve my short-term vision of success? What about my long-term definition of success?

Application

Let's start with revising your PSP. First, add "Intentional Growth" to your priority list. This will serve as a weekly reminder to intentionally look for opportunities for growth every day.

In Chapter 2, you identified tasks/activities/meetings that deserved your attention and added them to your calendar, and then in Chapter 4, you set an intention every day to create value at your maximum capacity in all your interactions. In this chapter, you ensure you grow at your maximum capacity in all your interactions.

How can you grow at your maximum capacity in all your interactions?

First and foremost, before you begin your workday, meeting, conversation, or new experience, set an intention to grow at your maximum capacity. This will ensure that you move from your current growth trajectory to a transformational growth trajectory.

Here are a few ideas that will help you.

Step Outside Your Comfort Zone

Start thinking about an assignment that you could take next that will push you outside your comfort zone—one that will push you to the edge of your current competence, one for which you don't have all the skills needed, one that scares you, one in which you've no idea whether you can succeed at or not, *and* one in which you'll learn relevant and marketable skills that will prepare you for your longer-term vision of success. Use connectors to get introductions to compete for such roles if necessary.

When seeking such roles, I recommend the following:

- Use the rubber band rule to stretch yourself to a point of tension, but never breakage. If you stretch a rubber band by only 20 percent, it's still loose and wobbly; there's a lot of unused potential. However, if you stretch that rubber band by 80 or 90 percent, you've got useful tension. In two to three months after taking on a new role or challenge, you should feel less and less stretched. If you aren't feeling that and are convinced that the role isn't right for you, find one that is. Remember, no decisions are irreversible.

- Know which of your current competences will create value for the role.
- Trust in your ability to learn new competences.
- Know that you don't have to figure everything out on your own. You can and should rely on your mentors, colleagues, and others for help.
- There's no such thing as failure; it's all about growth for future success.

Every time you're challenged, ask yourself, "What can I learn from this?" With this approach and attitude, you'll never allow challenges to overwhelm you; instead, you'll keep growing and moving forward. Frankly, if you're not being challenged in a job, you're not growing at your maximum capacity.

When you take on such roles, you'll realize just how capable you are. You'll also uncover more strengths, learn new skills, discover what you enjoy and don't enjoy. You will also learn what your weaknesses and limitations are. All this self-knowledge will enable you to make better choices in the future.

At the end of such assignments reflect upon and internalize your growth. Add the new competences you gained to your list of your current competences. Recognize that you're no longer the person who started the assignment and that you've grown exponentially. That recognition of your ability to navigate discomfort and grow when you get pushed outside your comfort zone will give you the confidence to push yourself further outside your comfort zone over and over again to create an upward spiral for growth so you can realize your maximum potential.

Move to a High-Growth Sector

If you're in a position and a sector that enables you to intentionally grow at your maximum capacity, great! If not, I recommend you start looking for positions in a growth sector that increase your chances of experiencing growth which will help you achieve your long-term definition of success.

Seek and Apply Feedback

You already know that feedback is an essential tool for growth, so I recommend setting time with your boss every quarter to receive feedback. Doing so ensures you won't be taken by surprise during your end-of-year reviews. Getting feedback early and consistently ensures that you can incorporate feedback throughout the entire year and improve your chances of success. Ask questions like, "What specific competences should I build or deepen that will help me improve my performance?" or "Can you provide some feedback for growth so I can improve my performance?"

You can also ask for feedback from your peers, employees, mentors, sponsors, or anyone else you truly respect and admire.

For example, after an important project or meeting in which you presented, stated an idea, or led a conversation, ask how you can improve. A question as simple as, "I want to improve my (insert specific skills)." Open questions like "Would you be so kind as to provide me with feedback so I can improve?" might help you uncover blind spots. Try to obtain feedback face-to-face as opposed to via electronic communication so you can ask for clarification if necessary.

Seeking sincere feedback and following through will help you build and deepen relationships with whoever provides the feedback. Remember what we learned earlier: Feedback is a rare gift. Treat it as such, and thank the person who delivered it.

Commit to Lifelong Learning

Set aside time for other learning in ways that work best for you. In addition to that treat every experience, whether it's a one-on-one conversation or a meeting, as an opportunity to learn and grow. Before every important meeting or interaction, take a moment to ask yourself, "What can I learn from this experience?" And at the end of each day, ask yourself, "How can I apply what I learned today?" Remember, the key is to learn for the sake not just of gaining knowledge, but for applying that knowledge to help you grow.

Your capacity to learn and to grow professionally and personally is limitless.

As you start executing on your strategy of Intentional Growth, you will seek growth in all your interactions. Every single day you'll intentionally grow, and all this incremental growth will get compounded over time and become transformational. You'll also consistently and proactively step outside your comfort zone to expand your competence and confidence. Your growth will increase your value creation, impact, and influence—all of which will move you closer to your definitions of success.

Reflection and Celebration

During your weekly reflection time, ask yourself the following questions:

- What growth did I experience this week?
- Did I grow at my maximum capacity?

If the answer to the second question is no, course-correct without beating yourself up. You can't belittle yourself to greatness. It's important to focus on progress and not on perfection. If you need a reminder, set a calendar reminder for every few hours, telling you to intentionally grow at your maximum capacity to ensure you don't fall back to autopilot.

No matter what, congratulate yourself for your answer to the first question, because that's growth you did experience. Reflect upon your growth, be grateful for the opportunity, and celebrate yourself for focusing on your growth. This process will motivate you to grow more the following week. Your daily and weekly incremental growth will create an upward spiral for growth and become transformational over time.

Over time you will master this strategy and Intentional Growth will become a habit.

SET YOUR INTENTIONS

Promise yourself:

- I will seek to grow at my maximum capacity each day.
- I will pursue assignments that push me outside my comfort zone.
- I will learn what I can from every experience and pursue the next experience more prepared because I know there is no such thing as failure—only lessons learned.

6

INTENTIONAL RELATIONSHIPS

I've learned that people will forget what you said, people will forget what you did, but people will never forget how you made them feel.

MAYA ANGELOU

THE SIXTH strategy that will help you show your worth and emerge as a leader is Intentional Relationships. Intentionally building and deepening meaningful relationships will not only accelerate and support your success at every level of your career, but also make your career journey richer, more fulfilling, and more fun. When you show up to work every day with an intention of building and deepening relationships, it becomes a game changer.

Alex Haley, a renowned American author, kept a photograph of a turtle sitting on a fence post in his office. He said, "When you see a turtle on a fence post, you know it had some help getting there." I love this photo and the meaning behind it because I believe the same. I can tell you with certainty that without my relationships, I would not have become the leader I am today—and becoming a senior executive might not have been possible.

Professional relationships weren't the only connections that helped elevate me; my personal relationships have shaped me into who I am today and give meaning to my life, too. Growing up in a community-centered environment, surrounded by my extended family, I learned the importance of relationships at a very young age—as you read in earlier chapters, without them I might not have obtained a college degree.

I was great at forming personal relationships, but as soon as I started my career, I struggled with building professional relationships, much like many of the women I mentor. It's hard to relate with coworkers when no one in your workplace looks like you, but you must learn to find some common ground.

INSIGHT

How you see people is a reflection of how you see yourself.

As you read in Chapter 4 on Intentional Value Creation, when I first started working, I compared myself with my coworkers and was fixated on our differences. It was only after I recognized my own worth and felt good about the value I created that I realized what mattered was not my appearance, education, or experience, but my capabilities and my ideas which translated into value I could contribute to the success of my organization. Collaborating around value creation became the common ground upon which I started building my professional relationships. Instead of seeing people's appearances, I focused on the value my coworkers were contributing and the value I was contributing—that became our point of connection.

I learned that we are more similar than we are different, but because the differences are visible and the similarities aren't always as easy to find, it's important to intentionally look for them. I also learned that while common ground is a great way to start building your relationships, respecting and appreciating our differences is necessary for creating combined unique value and leads to deep and sustained relationships. You must understand that as humans we tend to generalize and stereotype people based on their external appearances. This doesn't serve us well in building meaningful relationships. Each one of us is unique, and each one of us is evolving all the time. Recognition, respect, and appreciation of this fact is key in building meaningful, authentic relationships.

The way you make people feel in every interaction forms your relationships. Your interactions can build and deepen your relationships or weaken them. As so beautifully expressed in the Maya Angelou quotation at the beginning of this chapter, "people will never forget how you made them feel." So become very intentional about how you want others to feel when you interact with them.

Every relationship matters—no matter how big or small; this includes relationships with your peers, extended teams, clients, line of management, employees, mentors, mentees, sponsors, and other stakeholders.

However, there are four categories of relationships that are especially critical to help you emerge as a leader, and that's where we'll focus our attention in this chapter: *your boss*, *your peers*, *your mentors*, and *your sponsors*.

But before we get into individual relationships, it's essential that you ensure trust and integrity in all your relationships by doing the following:

- Always be truthful, sincere, and transparent.
- Follow through and keep your commitments.
- Be consistent in your behavior.
- Don't make assumptions.

- Clarify expectations so you avoid heartaches and headaches later on.
- Seek to understand others and ask clarifying, thought-provoking questions.
- Develop effective listening skills.
- Pay attention to your choice of words.
- Don't take things personally, and give others the benefit of the doubt—they might be having a bad day.
- Keep all conversations in strict confidence.

And now let's turn our attention to the first of the four categories of relationships.

YOUR RELATIONSHIP WITH YOUR BOSS

The single most important relationship of your career is the one with your immediate boss. This is the relationship that will make or break your career. Even though you might think you work for an organization, the reality is that you work for your boss. Even if everyone at your company aside from your boss is impressed with your work, your career success and your job experience will be highly dependent on your relationship with your immediate boss.

Your boss is a decision maker in every promotion, every assignment, and every award you may or may not receive. Your boss will determine your salary, your other compensation including stock options, your performance appraisal, your retention—and everything else that has to do with your career. Your boss will represent you to her or his boss and all the other senior executives your boss interacts with. Your boss has a front row seat to witness your performance and can play the role of a mentor or coach to help you improve your performance. Your boss can help you emerge as a leader—or not; that all depends on the relationship you have with her or him.

While both sides are responsible to make the relationship work, I encourage you to be proactive and intentional about building this relationship. An enlightened leader will take the initiative to build a relationship with you, but you can't depend on that happening.

Your success is tied to helping your boss (and your organization) succeed, and you should look for every opportunity to help make that a reality. Your boss's job is also to help you succeed, as your boss's success is tied to your success; however, the success of your boss can be achieved by the success of your peers, so your boss isn't as dependent on you as you are on your boss. Invest in your boss's success, and give your boss a reason to invest in yours.

Intentionally building a trusted win-win *professional* relationship with your immediate boss should be your number one priority. I emphasize professional relationship and not a personal relationship for a reason: Your relationship with your boss must be centered on your mutual success at work. Don't strive to make your boss your personal friend—and definitely not your personal therapist. Your boss isn't someone you should go to for help resolving your personal issues or conflicts. You must do that on your own or find others to help you. Always remember that your boss will be your boss for a limited period of time, but what you share with your boss can't be unsaid, so be intentional about what you want to share. That being said, if you have a personal situation that's impacting your performance at work, you must let your boss know.

I'll provide guidance on how you can build a meaningful relationship with your boss in the Intentional Exercises section.

What You Think About Your Boss Matters

Although you have choices about who you work for, you may sometimes end up working for someone you didn't choose, so you must figure out a way to build this relationship.

Don't expect your boss to meet your definition of a perfect person: Find good in your boss, and focus on the strengths that make your boss successful at work. Always start with the belief that people mean well and are doing their best based on what they know—unless they prove you wrong.

I've worked with many women who struggle to connect meaningfully with their boss because they've formed a negative mental model of the person.

The basic building block of any relationship is what we think of the other person. What we think of others creates our mental model of them. And we view them based on the mental model we created.

Think about this: If someone you like and someone you don't like both say the exact same thing to you, how will you take what each has said? Let me share a story with you to illustrate the impact of inadvertently creating a negative mental model and then changing it.

A mentee of mine came to the United States as a refugee and was the first person in her family to obtain a college degree. She landed her dream job right out of college with a company she had an internship with, and she was very excited to start her career.

> **INSIGHT**
>
> The mental model you form of an individual will define your relationship with that person.

I met her two months after she started her new job. She loved her job, and she especially liked her boss, who had hired her as both an intern and a full-time employee. One month later, she sat with me and began complaining about her new boss—the one she loved left the company just a week after we met.

She started her conversation with, "I really, really miss my old boss, and I don't like working for my new boss." She then explained that her boss wasn't friendly, never smiled, and had no prior management experience. She also told me that she felt like this role was above her head and that her boss didn't like her.

It was clear to me that she had already formed a negative mental model of her boss—and she viewed all her boss's actions through that lens.

"I know you really liked your old boss and miss her," I told her. "However, having new bosses is very common, and you'll have to learn to work with her. Give her a chance," I said. "We all have to start somewhere." I shared with her how much I had to learn about being a good leader when I first stepped into the role.

She responded: "I get that, and it's not just about her experience level. She doesn't like me. She wants to see me fail," she complained. "She keeps giving me tough assignments."

I asked her to explain why she thought her boss didn't like her, and she said, "I'm pretty sure it's because I'm colored. No one on my team looks like me."

I asked her if it was possible that her assumption was wrong, to which she responded, "It may be, but I'm pretty sure, and when I talk to my friends about her, they agree with me."

I then asked her, "Do you get the assignments done?"

She responded, "Of course I do."

I asked, "Do they stretch you and grow your competence?"

"Oh, you've got no idea!" she said emphatically. "I really struggle, but eventually I figure them out. Sometimes I even go to her to ask her for help, but she keeps pushing me to figure it out by myself. She doesn't help me. I'm telling you, she doesn't like me."

I then asked her: "Could it be possible that she's pushing you because she knows you have potential? Because she knows you're capable of getting them done and done well?"

She gave me a strange look, then hesitantly said, "Maybe, even though it's hard. I guess she knows I'll get it done, so she keeps giving me tougher and tougher assignments."

I smiled and looked my mentee in the eye and said: "I think she's actually doing you a favor. If I were you, I'd consider such assignments a gift for growth. When she gives you assignments that challenge you, make sure you let her know that you appreciate her confidence in your ability to get them done. And once you complete them, thank her for the opportunity for growth. Make sure she knows what you learned. She needs to recognize your growth."

"Oh, I don't know about that. If I do that, she'll give me tougher assignments."

"Yes, and that's great. It means she trusts you'll get them done." I continued: "While I understand that she's new and perhaps still learning how to be an effective leader, look for her strengths and give her the benefit of the doubt. She's doing the best she can. I think if you change the way you think about her, you'll see her differently."

I recommended that she use her Power Quotient to change her thoughts about her boss just like she changed her own self-limiting thoughts and give her boss a chance since this job was my mentee's dream job. I told her she should give it her best shot to build a relationship with her boss, and after that, if her boss truly isn't the person she wants to work with, she should look for another job within or outside the company.

I could tell by the way she thanked me for that advice that she wasn't sure I was right. But because she knew me well enough to know that I had her best interest at heart, she decided to give my advice a try.

In time, she shifted the lens through which she viewed her boss, and as a result her interactions with her boss changed. She started looking at those assignments as a gift for growth instead of her boss's desire to see her fail, and that changed everything.

She started enjoying her assignments instead of resenting them. She also started noticing her boss's strengths. As a result, they built a trusted win-win relationship, and within a year, my mentee was the first person her boss promoted.

Such is the power of the mental models you create. Remember, these are *your* mental models, which means you have the power to change them to help you build better relationships.

When Your Boss Doesn't Deserve You

Having said all that, I want you to know that you own the decision to keep your boss or not. There may be times where fundamental differences become impossible to overlook in a relationship with a boss. After giving your absolute best effort to build a relationship with this person, if the person proves not to be deserving of your relationship, you should look for another job within or even outside your organization. That may sound dramatic, but it's that critical.

INSIGHT

You own the power to choose your boss.

Twenty months into my first role as an executive, our team was restructured, and I got a new boss whose core values and leadership principles were not aligned with mine. I simply couldn't respect him enough to even begin to build a relationship. Within three months of his becoming my boss, I found another position within IBM—the only time I chose not to build a relationship with my boss during my 29-year career.

The reality is, you own the power of choosing whether or not to work for your boss. You should always be in control and never feel stuck with a boss who doesn't deserve you.

YOUR RELATIONSHIPS WITH YOUR PEERS

Your peers are the people who are on the same level of the organizational hierarchy as you. A relationship with a peer is a relationship of equals. Peers collaborate with each other and also support each other.

These relationships are the ones that will make your day-to-day work more enjoyable. Your peers make you look forward to work each day because you enjoy working with them. They're the people who'll cover for you when you need to take time off. They could also be the people who'll report to you when you get promoted and help you to be successful.

Your peers could also turn into your mentors, bosses, and sponsors; and when you cultivate your relationship with someone at a peer level, that relationship will grow as you both advance in your careers.

My peer relationships throughout my career not only have made my career more enjoyable but have also given me a sense of belonging. I've never worked in a job where my achievements were dependent on my contribution alone. I've always needed (and luckily received) support from my peers to make my success possible.

Every relationship requires a time investment, and peer relationships are no different. If you aren't intentional about building and nurturing peer relationships, it can hurt your performance. Why? Because when you don't intentionally build your peer relationships, your peers will only collaborate with you because they have to, not because they want to. That difference impacts their engagement, your mutual experience, and the outcome of your work together.

And it's not all about success, either; it's about friendship, too. Your peers can be your friends at work—unlike the other three relationships—so be sure to invest the time and effort to intentionally build and nurture your peer relationships.

YOUR RELATIONSHIPS WITH YOUR MENTORS

The mentor-mentee relationship is one of the most popular topics I'm asked about—and the most misunderstood. Almost every conference and magazine will discuss the importance of mentors, as they should. Having the right mentors at the right time can significantly help your career success.

Let's start with a basic understanding of the role of a mentor: A mentor is someone who can lend you her or his expertise for your career success, inspire you to achieve more success, help you navigate your career, guide you, and learn from and share ideas to give you a fresh perspective. A mentor can offer you understanding when you're struggling, confidence when you're in doubt, and celebration as you make progress. A mentor can make connections for you, have a lasting impact that allows you to experience growth, help you take on new challenges, see potential in you, and open your eyes to the unwritten, unspoken rules of business. A mentor can teach you "hard business skills" as well as soft skills.

It's not about how many or how few mentors you have or how frequently you meet with them; it's about the impact your mentors can have on your career, who your mentors are, and the quality of your relationships with your mentors.

Why Do You Want a Mentor?

Before you get a mentor, you should think carefully about why you want a mentor and what you'd like to get out of this relationship. This is an important first step. If you want to emerge as a leader, you must focus on finding mentors to help you with business expertise that will enable you to deliver value at a higher level and also to help you with leadership skills that will set you up for success.

Still another great reason to look for a mentor is so you can get help in deciding your next roles. Whatever your reasons are, be very clear with your "why." The clearer you are, the more likely you'll derive maximum value from your relationship.

Understanding Different Types of Mentors

Once your why for having a mentor is clear, you'll need to start looking for the right mentors. But before you get to that point, it's important to understand different types of mentors you can work with. Let's take a look at some of the most common, but not always obvious, types of mentors.

Also, remember that since mentors play so many different roles, you'll have many mentors throughout your career and multiple mentors at any given time, because they serve different needs.

Long-Term Mentors

Long-term mentors are people you want as your mentors for two or more years. (Long-term mentors can become sponsors over time, too.) They not only will provide support and guidance when needed, but will also be consistently aware of your performance and potential. You should typically speak with them at least once a quarter. Their level in the organization doesn't matter. If they're at a higher level than your boss, your association with them will carry a lot of weight.

Short-Term Mentors

Short-term mentors provide expertise, support, advice, and guidance when you're going through a challenging situation or you want to improve your performance. These types of mentors are great when you have a new role or project and are in uncharted territory. Find someone that has successfully done that role or worked on a similar project. This person can be a partner to bounce ideas off and brainstorm with.

A short-term mentor doesn't have to be someone you work with for a new project or role, only! It could be any situation where help from someone else would make you more successful. The important thing is to find someone who has "been there, done that" successfully so you don't have to reinvent the wheel and can learn from the person's experience. Short-term mentors can also lend credibility with your boss for something you're trying for the first time, and you're able to mention their guidance.

Typically, these relationships last around a year or less, which is around the same time you'll feel comfortable with the situation they've been helping you with. And some short-term mentors can evolve into long-term mentors if the relationship remains meaningful for both parties after the short-term need is fulfilled.

Personal Mentors

Personal mentors are people you go to for personal situations. They can be friends or family you respect and admire. They're typically people you want to learn from because they inspire you. You should be able to share your personal struggles with them in confidence. They can be your personal support system. No matter your specific reason for wanting personal mentors, I highly recommend you invite them into your life.

Connector Mentors

Connector mentors help you make connections. Whether you're looking for a new role inside your organization, applying for a new job, hoping to find short-term mentors, or wanting introductions to people in different parts of your business, connector mentors can help. Because of their reputation as connectors, when they introduce you to someone new, their connection will also carry the weight of their credibility. Connectors can be at any level in the organization; just be sure they're credible and have access to people you want to be connected to.

Where to Find a Mentor

Now that you know about different types of mentors you can work with, it's time to decide where to find them.

First evaluate what your needs are and make a list of the best possible candidates that could help you with what you need. Think of all the people that can lend the expertise you are currently seeking, and then get to work looking for them where you have maximum chances of finding the right fit.

You can do this by having a conversation with your boss on why you need a mentor. Know that your boss is invested in your success so asking them for help is a win-win. Whether your boss mentors you directly or suggests a mentor to you, your boss holds a good deal of knowledge and expertise. Your boss most likely knows and is connected to people who've had a similar job to yours and performed so well that they're at the same level as your boss.

Another great way to find a mentor is to join an employee resource group (ERG) if your organization has one. Make it a priority to become a member and an active participant. ERGs are voluntary, employee-led groups that foster a diverse, inclusive workplace aligned with organizational mission, values, goals, business practices, and objectives. ERGs are a great place to find mentors, because they're often filled with people you can relate to. Instead of just participating in those meetings, volunteer to help.

If your organization doesn't have such groups, take the initiative to start one, even if it's very small. It will make you stand out, while also helping your career and the careers of other women who join. Support each other and make it fun; invite speakers to attract other women. Heck, invite me!

Women's groups or other diversity groups outside your organization are also a great place to find mentors. Volunteer at those events to increase your chances to engage with other women at a deeper level.

Industry events are also a great way to engage with other women and find mentors.

Another way to find a mentor is through common acquaintances. The mutual person you know must have a solid relationship with both parties to feel comfortable in making introductions.

Some women have also found mentors by initiating a relationship and sending them a short note through email or any other communication tool such as a LinkedIn message. If you choose this method, be sure you get their attention by the way you engage. Make your message personal and sincere.

I've also worked with women who've struck up a conversation on an airplane, during a business trip, on a vacation, and even at a spa or their gym and found an unexpected mentor. The point is, you can find potential mentors anywhere as long as you're intentionally looking and you know your why.

How to Connect with Potential Mentors

Once you've determined who your potential mentors could be and what role they could play, strategize about how you can get a first meeting with them. I'm a firm believer in earning mentorship. Good mentors are busy so you must give your mentors a reason to make you a priority and invest time in you. Know that their time is at a premium, and determine why they should prioritize spending their attention on you. With that being said, know that most people want to be mentors and gain a lot by being a mentor, so as long as you're deserving of their mentorship, they'll welcome the opportunity to be your mentor.

Send them a short communication asking them for no more than 30 minutes, and be very specific about what you need and why. Also mention why they're the best to provide you the support you need. Essentially, give them a reason why they should invest their attention in you. Never use vague language or cookie-cutter emails. These won't work. And if they don't know you, use a connector to make an introduction to improve your chances.

If they don't respond, understand that they've got other priorities and move down your list. They should want to be your mentor in order for this relationship to work.

How Frequently Should You Meet with Your Mentor?

The frequency of your meetings and the duration of your relationship will vary based on your needs.

At the end of your first meeting with your potential mentor, if you believe that you'd benefit by meeting this person on a regular basis, ask if that would be a satisfactory arrangement. Jointly agree on a cadence and duration of your meetings. Oftentimes, the frequency and the duration of your meetings are determined as the relationship progresses.

Sometimes just a one-hour meeting with your mentor can have a profound impact on your career—as it did for me.

In December 2012, a year after Ginni Rometty became the CEO of IBM, I was asked to review my strategy for the IBM/Microsoft Global Alliance with her and her strategy team, which consisted of IBM's most senior leaders globally.

Prior to my getting the role, the relationship between IBM and Microsoft was very contentious based on past experiences. Many senior IBM executives viewed Microsoft as their main competitor, and most did not trust the company. The outcome of this meeting could be the continuation of or the end of my role.

I'd be making a different kind of presentation than I was used to and to a very different audience than I was used to. Instead of just presenting my strategy, I needed to get buy-in from them to continue my role. I wasn't sure how to prepare and present at this meeting. None of my current mentors had any expertise in this area.

I researched all the members of Ginni's strategy team and learned that Jon Iwata, IBM's chief marketing officer, was on the team. I'd known Jon for about 10 years. As IBM's senior-most Asian executive, he was active in our Asian ERG. He was also our executive sponsor for IBM's Asian Executives leadership team, and I was one of the co-leads. I had been an active participant of this group for many years and had met him several times. I sent him an email asking for an hour of guidance on how to structure my presentation. He became my mentor for one hour, and in that hour, he gave me invaluable guidance which I will share with you as that could come in handy for you one day, too.

He advised that for the 50-minute meeting I shouldn't have more than five charts. Jon's reasoning was this: "You want the leaders to pay attention to you, not read your charts. If you must have visuals, use them to support and illustrate what you have to say. Don't stand there and read charts to them. Otherwise, just send them the materials."

That made sense. He further explained: "The first is the most important chart, as it sets the stage. This chart must address the elephant in the room. If it doesn't, you'll lose them."

Jon's suggestion was logical—demonstrate empathy, anticipate the greatest objections in the room, and frame them as three simple questions at the outset:

1. What's in it for us?
2. What's in it for them?
3. What's in it for our clients?

That was straightforward, but his next piece of advice wasn't. "After you've articulated those three points, stop and ask for their thoughts," he said. "Don't move to the next slide, and don't answer their questions yourself. Invite others to engage."

I didn't understand this. I'd been invited to make a presentation to the senior management of the company. This was my chance. I wanted to demonstrate my strategic thinking, my smarts, that I'd done my homework and come up with brilliant recommendations. So I asked Jon, "Why shouldn't I answer questions myself?"

He asked, "How will you know your presentation is successful?"

I said, "IBM continues to invest in keeping an alliance with Microsoft."

He said, "Yes. But to achieve that, your role is to frame the discussion and get them to engage. Some will fight the idea. Others will say why an alliance is the right thing to do. They need to convince each other, as peers, that this is a good idea. Otherwise, they'll sit back and listen to you, and then you'll get a few polite questions and be thanked. And then absolutely nothing will happen. Your goal is to get senior management to do something, not for you to get praised for a good presentation."

So I asked, "I don't do anything other than moderate a discussion?"

And his response: "Answer questions directed to you. Be concise. Be clear. Keep it simple. That will convey confidence and conviction in your point of view. But keep them talking and debating among themselves. You're framing and guiding a dialogue."

His guidance was nerve-racking, but exactly what I needed. I thanked him profusely for his time.

The night before the meeting, I flew to Armonk, New York. The next day was a typical cold winter day, and everything was blanketed in snow. I didn't want to take a chance with the icy roads, so I arrived at IBM headquarters an hour and a half before my meeting.

I was more nervous than usual. I needed to shake off my nerves. Walking in the woods is a great way for me to calm down, but it was too icy outside, and I wasn't dressed for a walk; so, instead, I started walking around the hallway of our corporate headquarters, where there is a timeline tracing the history of computing and IBM's pioneering role. I came to the era of the personal computer: 1981, when IBM built the first IBM Personal Computer.

My thoughts carried me back to my story I shared with you in Chapter 1 about the *PC World* magazine, I read in 1981 about the IBM Personal Computer and how it would be a game changer for computing. The article also mentioned that there were plenty of high-paying jobs for people with degrees in computer science. This was what had sparked my career in computer science. And here I was, 31 years later, about to present to the CEO of IBM itself. Deep gratitude overflowed from my heart, replacing my nervousness.

As the meeting began, I introduced myself and my role, after which I put up the first slide. As Jon had advised, I took them through three bullet points. Then I stopped and asked their thoughts.

Silence.

It lasted two minutes, but it was the most unnerving two minutes of my career. It seemed like an hour. Just as Jon had suggested, I didn't move to the next slide. I made eye contact with every single person, soliciting feedback with my eyes.

Finally, someone spoke. He raised some concerns. The salesperson in me was tempted to jump in and allay his concerns immediately. But since he hadn't asked me directly, I said nothing. Instead, I scanned the room again, inviting others to participate. Pin-drop silence. But the second time it was slightly easier to withstand. After a minute, the next senior executive chimed in, also expressing concern. After that, conversation flowed freely. Most people expressed concerns.

After about 20 minutes, one senior executive joined the conversation, providing perspective on why we should have this alliance. His perspective carried a great deal of weight, and that turned the tide of the conversation. Because of that moment, many others chimed in with a willingness to continue the alliance.

Such is the power of an hour of mentorship. Sixty minutes with Jon was all I needed to literally save my job and get buy-in from senior executives whose support I needed. You don't get second chances for meetings like this, so you must do everything in your power to prepare and ask for help from the best possible individual.

When you're trying your very best, when you've demonstrated past success, when you've built a stellar brand, when you're stretching yourself and need someone else's expertise, I've found that most people, no matter how high up they are in an organization, will make time for you. They were all once in your position and had people invest in them. And please remember one more thing: Exposure to very high-level executives can backfire if you're not prepared to use their valuable time as effectively as possible.

When you're in a situation in which you need specific expertise and guidance for a high-stakes meeting or an important decision, you can seek mentorship for an hour from the best-possible person. You've earned the right to ask for such expertise by executing and mastering the strategies in this book.

YOUR RELATIONSHIPS WITH YOUR SPONSORS

Let's start with the basics: What is a sponsor exactly?

A sponsor is an influential leader in your organization and is typically two levels higher than you. These people are the decision makers or the influencers who may be at the table when you're one of the candidates being considered for a high-visibility assignment, a promotion, or a new job; and if they aren't at the table, their recommendation to those who are would mean you'd be seriously considered. They use their strong influence to advocate for you in many settings.

They put their credibility on the line to advocate for you, so you must give them reasons to be your sponsor. The more they know you and have witnessed your performance under different business situations and over the long term, the more likely they are to become your sponsor.

Having a sponsor raises your profile within the entire organization, and especially with your boss, peers, and mentors.

A sponsor relationship is more difficult than any other relationship and it's often the relationship that keeps women away from the highest levels in the organization.

Getting a sponsor is difficult because sponsors are very busy, there are a limited number of them, and many people are vying for their attention. You' will need a stronger case to make sure you' are deserving of their attention. As you execute and master your eight intentional strategies, you'll be showing more and more of your worth to everyone you interact with including potential sponsors—this will help you earn their sponsorship. Potential sponsors will become interested in sponsoring you as they will see the potential of a future leader in you.

Remember, they're also motivated to be your sponsor, as it makes them look good when they recommend a great candidate. In many organizations that are focused on increasing women (and especially women of color) in leadership roles, senior executives are given incentives to sponsor women for leadership roles—sponsoring you is a terrific win-win.

Over the years, as I've been promoted to various leadership positions, I've gained a deep appreciation for the gravity of two things: how you're known and who knows you. I've participated in many meetings where executive-level promotion decisions are made, and I've witnessed the critical need for a sponsor in such decisions. Everyone being considered for the role is a high achiever and has the potential to get the job done. The positions are few, and the competition is between the best of the best. What becomes a differentiator is the person who knows and advocates for the candidate—the sponsor. Every woman I know who has made it to an executive role has had a sponsor advocating for her. While you might advance at lower levels without sponsorship, sponsors play a crucial role if you want to become an executive so seeking sponsors is necessary.

All the executives in your organization are potential sponsors. Whenever you get an opportunity to interact with them, intentionally leave an impression that will allow them to remember you as someone who has the potential to be a future leader. You never know when or how often your paths will cross again.

Star performers that you see getting frequent promotions and those that have strong relationships with senior executives are also great potential sponsors. They can be at the same level as you or even lower today, but they're moving up the ladder, perhaps even faster than you. Start cultivating relationships with them now, and make sure they're aware of your achievements and your ambitions. These relationships will evolve over time, and you'll earn their sponsorship over time. Keep in mind that your mentors and bosses can turn into your sponsors over time as they move up the corporate ladder and become senior executives, too.

How I Earned Sponsorship

Let me share how Susan Whitney and Rodney Adkins became my sponsors. I met them at different times in my career under different circumstances.

———

After the first meeting I had with Susan (which I shared in Chapter 1), I sent her an email when I joined sales to let her know how our conversation sparked a fire in my belly to unlock my potential. She responded right away, which encouraged me to send her an email every quarter with my achievements. I knew she was busy, so I kept my emails very short and to the point. I also sent her an email when I bought my house and when Sophia was born. She responded to each of my emails.

She was based in New York and I was in Minneapolis and then Seattle, so we didn't get to see each other often. After she got promoted to a senior executive in our hardware business, she was a key-note speaker at our annual sales conference. When I heard this news, I was ecstatic, as I'd get to see her again after two years! I made sure I said hello to her even though I had to wait in line for 30 minutes to get her attention. She'd made such an impression on me that I didn't want her to forget me. We had a great conversation for about five minutes.

Two years after our second in-person meeting, I asked her if I could list her name as my mentor when I filled out my performance appraisal, to which she said, "I would be honored." I then started asking for 30-minute in-person meetings when we were at the same annual conference, and I continued sending her my quarterly performance updates.

She watched me and my performance closely over the years and remained engaged. I knew she was extremely busy. I respected her time immensely and never took it for granted. Most years, if she wasn't at our sales conference, I would speak to her on the phone just once for only 15 to 30 minutes. Knowing that I could go to her for guidance whenever I needed it was enough for me, and being able to list her as my mentor during my performance appraisals helped me gain credibility with my boss, as Susan was at a much higher level in the organization and very well respected. My association with her carried significant weight.

As Susan advanced in her career, she became a senior executive in our hardware business, and she naturally evolved into my sponsor. And eight years after knowing each other, she advocated for me when I was competing for my second promotion. When that happened, it became even more important for me to succeed in that role, because I knew she had put her credibility on the line for me. Letting her down was not an option.

As I succeeded in that role, we deepened our relationship. Because of my previous mentoring relationship with Susan, she also continued to be my mentor whenever I needed any advice or guidance throughout my career.

After that position, I was hoping she would sponsor me for an executive role in our hardware business, but instead, she encouraged me to move into the services division, as you read in Chapter 5, which created a pathway for me to get promoted to an executive. Our relationship continues to this day.

I met Rodney Adkins nine years before he became my sponsor, when he was the general manager of our hardware business. I engaged him in some of my toughest, most competitive, and most complex deals when I was a competitive sales representative. (I'll talk about this in detail in Chapter 8 on Intentional Promotion.)

I received multiple awards from him over several years as a sales representative, first line sales manager, and second line sales manager. Every time he presented me with an award, he became more and more aware of my capabilities and my success.

Seven years after meeting him, he invited me for a one-year growth assignment, as he describes in the Foreword of this book. I shadowed him for a year and learned how our company operates at the highest levels. This role gave me exposure to every senior executive at IBM. At the end of that year, his advocacy was instrumental in my receiving multiple offers for my first executive position. Later, he advocated for me for the high-stakes position of vice president of the IBM/Microsoft Global Alliance. In both instances, I was determined to succeed not just for myself but also for him because he'd put his credibility on the line for me.

I am deeply grateful for the significant role Susan and Rod have played in my career. They showed me firsthand the power of sponsors and mentors in my career. They have inspired me to sponsor and mentor hundreds of women. I am hoping to become your mentor through this book.

A STORY OF
INTENTIONAL RELATIONSHIPS

Jennifer DaSilva
President at Berlin Cameron

Jennifer is a president at Berlin Cameron, founder of Connect4Women, and a fellow board member at the United Nations Foundation's initiative Girl Up.

Jennifer's story is a great illustration of the fact that regardless of how high we rise in an organization, we all crave relationships to enrich our lives and careers. Here's her story.

In recent years, I've become known as an advocate for connecting women with other women—the "master connector," so to speak. I've written about it in publications, I've spoken about it on panels, and I've even gone so far as to create a network called Connect4Women that now has more than 300 members, all of whom are committed to helping other women through introductions and mentoring.

And maybe the most important thing I've learned in my adult life is that by being open and vulnerable with other women, by showing my imperfections, I can grow and become more connected as a result. It wasn't always that easy, though.

Let me back up for a minute—all the way to Los Gatos, California, in the *very* early 1980s. I'm an only child, so when I was a kid, my parents used to tease me about how I was held back in kindergarten because I was bad at sharing. Despite my lack of sharing prowess, even as a child I strove for connection. I was so enamored by the idea of being part of a group that at one point I asked my parents to take me to the Protestant church (we were Catholic), which, I heard, had a rock band and a community, and my parents said they'd drop me off. I never went as I wasn't ready at age 10 to go to church alone.

Then there was the constant pursuit of perfection. My mother was the type who "had it all" and made it look effortless: She owned her own business, had a family, was essentially a gourmet cook, and never seemed to gain a pound (she still looks fantastic in her seventies). I thought that I had to be perfect, too, which manifested itself in many ways—getting good enough grades to be at the top of my high school class, wearing the same turtleneck sweater in different colors all throughout college (which became something of a piece of armor), making sure I never had a single hair out of place in my perfectly coiffed bob. But instead of protecting me, this shield of perfection was turning people away.

As a young adult, I chose to go to Boston College, a Jesuit school, as I was still in search of the community that I'd built up in my mind. Even there, I had difficulties connecting (maybe now I realize it was the turtleneck-and-bob daily situation). It wasn't until I became a mother that I realized that I could never be "perfect"—that I needed to shed the mask of perfection that I'd spent 36 years building up, or it could break me. As I started to talk to other moms about my challenges and the stresses of motherhood, I started to find it more natural to connect. Vulnerability was the key to my story, and unlocking that power enabled me to foster deeper, more meaningful connections.

An Idea That Sparked a Community

When I came back from maternity leave, I felt like a new person and made a vow to myself to be as vulnerable at work as

I was with the moms in my network. From that point on, the doors started to open. I felt less afraid, and slowly but surely my work network started to build and change. I reached out to acquaintances, asked for coffee dates, and strove to meet one new person a week whether by a call or in person with a coffee or some wine. I also realized what was natural to me in these conversations was finding a way to weave this person into my network by connecting her with others. I was literally building the web/community that I strove for my entire life.

In March 2019, I was on the elliptical and had an idea. If I could connect four women a day, and each of them could connect four women a day, to form a support network, imagine how strong our network could become. Soon, Connect4Women was born. It's grown every year, with new initiatives (like Young Connectors and now a SheCovery Network for women looking for work during the pandemic).

I don't know what I would've done during the COVID-19 pandemic if it weren't for my support system. We helped each find jobs and ask for higher salaries, and we even cried together on Zoom calls when the pressures of the pandemic got to be too much. I let my guard down with these incredible women, which showed others that it's OK to have a bad day or ask for help. By being real and vulnerable with each other, we actually got stronger, together.

How You Can Get More Connected

Women often ask me for tips to build their own networks of strong, supportive women. Here's what I tell them:

Use the magic to fuel you. When you make a connection, you never know what could happen. Will it result in a business deal, a friendship, a relationship? Use the potential of that magical connection to inspire you. When I see the fruits of my labor play out in front of me at a conference or on social media, it's so worth it.

Remember the old adage "Practice makes perfect." Give yourself actionable, attainable goals; then stick to them. It's easier to take small steps than to bite off more than you can chew—"attainable" is key when building connections!

Be intentional. Explain your point of view on why two people should connect. It will help everyone to have some perspective, especially if you're introducing people in completely different industries.

Don't be afraid to make the ask. We've all been there: You really want an introduction, but you're too scared to ask for it. Leave that fear at the door: Just make sure you're being specific and thoughtful when you ask for an intro, which leads me to the next tip . . .

Remember that connecting is a two-way street. You know that friend who asks for favors all the time but never does anything in return? Yeah, uncool. The same goes for your network. You have to put in as much as you expect to get out.

Don't ghost. Seriously. If someone took the time to introduce you and then you just drop the ball, you both end up looking bad. Even if you simply follow up to say it isn't a great time for you to connect, that's better than no communication at all.

Once connected, open up and share your story. Tell your story in a way that's authentic to you. The more open you are to a new connection, the more open others will be to you.

INTENTIONAL EXERCISES

Now it's time to create and execute your strategy of Intentional Relationships. Let's start with Introspection, so you can gain knowledge of your current state of relationships. Then we'll move to the Application section, so you can apply the insights you learned in this chapter and intentionally start building meaningful relationships with your boss, peers, mentors, and sponsors. We'll wrap things up with Reflection and Celebration to look back, course-correct, and celebrate your successes of applying this strategy until you master it. Let's get started.

Introspection

Before we get into building your professional relationships, it's important to remember that your relationship with yourself will determine the quality of all your other relationships.

How you view yourself influences how you view others; in other words, your mental model of yourself will influence the mental models you create of others. So in order for you to build and maintain honest relationships with others, you must first be true to yourself by bringing your authentic, best, and sincere self to the relationship.

All the intentional introspection you've done in the previous chapters has given you a powerful basis of self-awareness and self-knowledge, so let's see where you currently stand in terms of relationships with yourself and the four relationships we've discussed in this chapter.

Answer these questions:

Relationship with Myself
- Am I kind to myself?
- Am I harsh on myself when I make mistakes?

- Do I forgive myself for my mistakes and move on?
- Am I quick to judge myself?

Relationship with My Boss

- How is my relationship with my boss?
- What personal and professional characteristics make my boss successful?
- What two things can I do to deepen my relationship with my boss?
- When was the last time I complimented my boss to her or his boss?
- When was the last time I expressed appreciation for my boss?
- What are my top two contributions to the success of my boss outside my job responsibilities?

Relationships with My Peers

- Which of my peers do I have a great relationship with? Which ones do I not?
- Do I celebrate their success sincerely?
- How well do I know them personally?
- Do I offer my expertise when they're struggling professionally?
- Do I offer my support when they're struggling personally?
- How often do I have lunch with each of them?
- Do I praise them generously when they help me in any way?

Relationships with My Mentors

- Do I have mentors? If so, who are they? If not, who can be my mentors?
- Do I think strategically about who my mentors should be and why?
- Do my mentors inspire me to achieve more success?

- Am I reaching high when looking for mentors?
- Do they challenge me and motivate me to bring out the best in me?

To determine if your current or future mentors are the right fit for you, answer the following questions:

- Will these people give me constructive feedback for improvement?
- Do they solve my problems and make decisions for me, or do they guide me?
- Do they make time for me and have my best interests at heart?
- Do they keep my confidential information to themselves?
- Are they happy to share their expertise and guidance with me?

Relationships with My Sponsors

- How often do I get to interact with leaders and/or executives who are at least two levels higher than me?
- Do I appreciate and lean into my uniqueness in the presence of senior executives? If not, why not?
- Who is the most senior person who knows me and my work well enough to be willing to vouch for my capabilities?
- Do I ensure that my interaction with a potential sponsor leaves an impression that I have the potential to be a leader?
- Who else can be a potential sponsor?

Application

Let's start with revising your PSP. First, add "Intentionally build meaningful relationships" to your priority list as a weekly reminder as relationships don't just happen, they require investment of time and effort.

First and foremost, before you begin your workday, meeting, conversation, or new experience, set an intention to build and/or deepen your relationships. This will ensure that you move from your current state of relationships to having strong and meaningful relationships with your boss, peers, mentors, and sponsors.

Next, let's walk through the specific steps to build those relationships.

Build a Meaningful Relationship with Your Boss

Seek to understand your boss and her or his leadership style as best you can. If you have a new boss, speak to someone who has worked with your boss before to get a jump start. Pay attention to everything your boss says in meetings or casual conversations, notice how your boss behaves, and observe how your boss interacts with higher-ups, peers, and your team. Seek to understand how your boss makes decisions—both big and small. Get to know your boss as a person. Some specific tactics that will help you are:

- Understand your boss's critical priorities and make them your own. Ask questions like, "What do you need that isn't being done?" and "How can I contribute in ways that go beyond my job description?"
- Find out how your boss will be evaluated, and create value that will lead to your boss's success.
- Aim to increase your boss's chances of success by asking thoughtful questions during meetings.
- When your boss helps you in a significant way, send an email to her or his boss to express your appreciation. Make it sincere and thoughtful: It should never be done in a hurry or be cookie-cutter. Copy your boss on it.
- When appropriate, share your values and whatever else you're comfortable sharing—for example, share about your family, favorite books, personal hobbies, upbringing, travels, etc.—to open up communication lines for your relationship.
- Build a trusted win-win relationship by making your boss your partner, both by sharing significant achievements and by

seeking help when things aren't going as expected. It can be hard to tell your boss that something isn't working as you had anticipated—however, the sooner you make your boss aware and ask for help, the better. Good news can wait, but bad news never should. Never have your boss be surprised by negative news.

- Praise your boss to others in her or his network, describing something specific your boss helped you with. Be sincere when you do this. Feedback about the praise from people in the network is music to your boss's ears.
- Appreciate your boss's time and interest in your success. Never take anything your boss does for you for granted, and always express appreciation for your boss's time and whatever else your boss does to help you become better.

Build Relationships with Your Peers

Seek to understand your peers, and look for the best in them. Get to know them enough to treat them the way they want to be treated.

- Always have their best interest at heart.
- Offer to help when they need you. Whether it's a specific skill you have for a project or backup when they're on vacation or have a family emergency, be there to support them.
- If they're having a difficult time in their personal lives, take time to show your support and take genuine interest.
- Sincerely celebrate their successes.
- Never engage in gossip or negative conversation about any of your peers—regardless of the situation.
- When forming new relationships with peers, seek to notice their personal and professional strengths and sincerely bring those strengths to their attention. Even better, mention those strengths in front of other peers and your boss.

- Always acknowledge and appreciate their role in your success as well as the success of your team.
- When any of your peers goes out of the way to help you in a significant way, make sure you mention the specifics to your boss. As a leader, I love it when one of my employees will mention another employee's role in providing help. I'm equally impressed with the individual praising their teammates as I am with the teammates being praised.

Build Relationships with Your Mentors

Start thinking about who can become your mentors and what roles they can play to help support your career success. Do some research on them, and get to know who they are and if they're the right fit for you. Once you've found your mentors, the following will help you build and deepen your relationship with them:

- Express appreciation for their time and interest in your success at the beginning of every meeting.
- Become comfortable being emotionally vulnerable when needed in order to create emotional resonance with your mentors. This includes working through your feelings of being intimidated by people who are higher up than you in the organization.
- Come prepared with an agenda and a list of questions focused on achieving success and learning business as well as leadership skills. Also ask them for their personal stories that are relevant to your situation.
- Praise your mentors to others in their network.
- Always be respectful of their time, and only ask for it when you truly need it. Some mentors might spend lots of time with you, others very little. The quantity of time isn't important; the value you receive in that time is.

- When you seek advice, follow through, implement it, and let them know you did the work. Show you're doing your part; even if it's difficult and even if it doesn't work as expected, they can help refine your approach. When they see you taking their advice seriously, they're inspired to remain engaged with you, further deepening your relationship.
- Seek ways to build trust. The tougher the challenges you overcome using their advice, the more respect and admiration you'll earn and the deeper your relationship will get.
- Always follow up and appreciate them when their advice/guidance works for you.

BE A MENTOR

Just as a mentor can play a critical role for your career, you can do the same for someone else by becoming a mentor. There's always another woman who could use your expertise. Find the person if she hasn't found you. It will not only be very fulfilling; it will give you an appreciation of a mentor-mentee relationship and help you become a better mentee.

Here are some ways you can become an effective mentor:

- Make the other person feel comfortable.
- Show enthusiasm for your mentee.
- Start with your mentee's agenda, never yours.
- Don't be anxious to persuade and convince, and don't push your point of view; just provide a perspective.
- Think about how your ideas will be received.
- Try to help the person come up with the right answer or best conclusion as opposed to giving it to her.

- Make the other her feel important, and do it sincerely.
- Talk in terms of the other person's interest.
- Give honest and sincere appreciation.
- Become genuinely interested in the person.
- Genuinely believe in the person; otherwise don't be a mentor.
- Treat her success as your success.
- Have her best interest at heart.
- Use the knowledge, skills, expertise, and experiences you have benefit her.

Attract Sponsors

Identify a minimum of two senior leaders in your organization who could be your potential sponsors. They must be influential and rising stars in your organization, and they don't have to necessarily be in your reporting structure.

You can meet sponsors by doing the following:

- Seek high-stakes assignments that create differentiated and outsized value for your organization.
- Lead projects that are so difficult that they can't be done without their engagement.
- Engage them in situations that are complex and difficult so they can witness your capabilities and contribution to the success of your organization firsthand.
- When they're in a meeting, volunteer to become a spokesperson for your team so they notice your ability to present ideas effectively. This can be in the form of a formal presentation or a conversation during a meeting. If you can't be the spokesperson, do your homework before the meeting

and come prepared to contribute meaningful value to the discussions.

- If they're visiting your city, ask your boss if you can spend some time with them to discuss your career aspirations. Tell your boss that you would like to cultivate a relationship with them so they can be your sponsors in the future.
- Work hard to win prestigious awards, and if they give you the award, follow up with a thank you email. After a few awards, they'll want to get to know you!
- Ask for advice or guidance when you know their specific expertise would help you. Just be sure you're always being exceptionally respectful of their time.

After you meet them, stay in touch by sending short emails once a quarter making them aware of your significant achievements. If they don't respond to your email, find other potential sponsors. They might not have the bandwidth to build a relationship with you. This relationship more than any other requires these people to be deeply interested and invested in you and your success.

Start building these relationships early in your career so by the time you're ready to get promoted to an executive position, they'll be at a much higher level and will have witnessed your leadership potential and consistent achievements for many years. This will result in them gladly putting their credibility on the line and advocating for you.

Reflection and Celebration

During your weekly reflection time, ask yourself the following questions:

- When did I seize opportunities to build or deepen meaningful relationships with my boss, peers, mentors, and sponsors?
- What else could I have done differently to build or deepen those relationships?

Learn and course-correct based on your answer to the second question. It's important to focus on progress and not on perfection. If you need a reminder, put a calendar reminder to build meaningful relationships every few hours to ensure you don't fall back to autopilot.

No matter what, congratulate yourself for the answers you wrote down for the first question, because those are the relationships you did nurture.

Be grateful and celebrate yourself for building meaningful relationships.

Your daily intention of building and maintaining relationships will become a habit over time, and you will have strong and meaningful relationships.

As you advance in your career and emerge as a leader, relationships will play a bigger and bigger role in your success. Once you advance two levels, intentionally look for women you can sponsor and help them emerge as leaders.

SET YOUR INTENTIONS

Promise yourself:

- I will honor every relationship I have.
- I will develop positive mental models of all the people I work with and give them the benefit of the doubt, unless they prove otherwise.
- I will intentionally seek to build and maintain meaningful relationships with my boss, peers, mentors, and sponsors.

7

INTENTIONAL LEADERSHIP BRANDING

*Character cannot be developed in ease and
quiet. Only through experience of trial and
suffering can the soul be strengthened,
ambition inspired, and success achieved.*

HELEN KELLER

THE SEVENTH strategy that will help you show your worth and emerge
as a leader is Intentional Leadership Branding. As I noted in the previous chapter, as I rose up the ranks of leadership, I got a much deeper
understanding and appreciation of the gravity of two things: how you're
known and who knows you. In this chapter, we will discuss the importance of how you are known. When you decide that you want to be
known as a leader and show up to work every day with the intention of
building and sustaining a leadership brand, you will become known as a
leader, even if you don't yet have a title of one.

Before we dive into your leadership brand, which is essentially
your personal brand that contains leadership attributes, let's take

a moment to talk about personal branding. Your personal brand is essentially what others say about you when you're not around. It's what others think when they hear your name.

Your personal brand consists of your business expertise as well as your personal attributes—it is your identity. Your personal brand plays a critical role at all stages of your career: It determines whether or not you get hired, promoted, and even approached for a better job. It influences your total compensation and the recognition you receive for your performance.

Your brand precedes you when you enter a room and goes with you across jobs. It dictates if and how people engage with you, which also impacts your performance. It also determines whether or not someone will invest in your success by becoming your mentor or sponsor.

Your personal brand is formed by the impression you leave behind in every interaction—whether it's a casual interaction, an in-person or virtual meeting, social media engagement, email exchange, a phone conversation, or any other means of communication. It's also formed by the way you approach situations and people, your attitude, your big decisions and small actions, your integrity, your values, what you stand for, and what you will and won't accept.

While your personal brand is formed by other people based on the impressions you leave, it's important to remember that it's *not* about agonizing over what people think about you. Instead, it's about intentionally becoming the person you want to be known as. And it's definitely not about pretending to be someone you aren't. That would be exhausting and inauthentic. Your brand has to be authentic in order for it to work long term.

LEADERSHIP MISUNDERSTANDINGS

When I talk about leadership branding, many women I work with believe that leadership is not for them mainly because they don't see leaders that look like them. They believe leadership is reserved for people who are "born to lead." That is not the case. Leadership is a learned behavior. When I tell them they're already leaders, they feel that's inauthentic. Do you feel that way? I can tell you with certainty that you already possess leadership skills.

How do I know that? Because you've taken an initiative to read this book. Whenever you take an initiative to change any aspect of your life or influence others in order to help them improve an aspect of their lives, you're demonstrating that you're already a leader. If you see potential in yourself or anyone else, you're a leader.

> **INSIGHT**
>
> **Know deeply that you have the capacity to lead.**

I did not see myself as a leader for many years after I started my career, and frankly, I should have recognized my leadership capabilities much earlier. In hindsight, I became a leader in third grade when I took an initiative to get good grades.

Everyone has the capacity to lead—including you. In addition to the leadership attributes you have today, you can intentionally learn whatever else you need to learn. I had to learn many of them myself, and I know you can, too. I continue to learn to this day and will never stop.

And, yes, some people can grasp some leadership skills more easily than others, and some skills will be harder for you to master than others, and that's OK. Don't ever get discouraged and believe that leadership is reserved for others and it isn't for you.

By executing and mastering the strategies in this book, you're already on your way to creating a leadership brand. You'll leave impressions that will earn you a branding of a high performer who consistently achieves or exceeds the value that's expected of you. You'll become known as someone who contributes toward the success of your boss as well as your organization. You'll become known for the unique value you create and the meaningful relationships you have. You'll become known as someone who consistently steps outside their comfort zone.

Every strategy will be reflected in your brand, and in turn, your brand will accelerate the execution and mastery of all your other strategies.

DEVELOPING YOUR LEADERSHIP BRAND

Just as companies invest time and resources to create a deliberate branding strategy, so must you. One of the first steps that companies take in developing brands is a two-parter: (1) establish their core purpose and (2) formulate their unique value proposition that will enable them to fulfill that purpose. Having a clearly defined and expressed purpose serves as an internal compass that guides their decision making and strategic direction. This unique differentiation is why customers will pick their product over another brand.

Personal brands work in the same way. Once your definition of success is to become a leader, you must intentionally build your leadership brand that will enable you to achieve that success. In Chapter 4 on Intentional Value Creation, I shared how I changed my brand from being a young woman who didn't speak up in meetings to someone who wouldn't let anyone interrupt her. In Chapter 5 on Intentional Growth, I shared how I intentionally changed my brand from being a leader who was brutally honest when providing feedback to a leader who provided feedback in a kind and firm manner. Now, I'd like to share a story of how I intentionally changed my branding from a subject matter expert to a leader.

INSIGHT

Self-awareness and an awareness of what's happening around you are key to leadership branding.

When I got my first promotion to a sales leader, the members of my team were eager to take me on client calls so I could witness them in action. I was eager to join them so I could add value for them with all my sales expertise. But this eagerness got the better of me, and when I went on my first two calls, I took over the meeting, just like

I used to do when I was a sales representative, thinking I was adding value. I failed to realize that I was actually embarrassing my team members in front of their clients and making it look like they weren't capable of conducting the meeting and solving problems themselves.

No one mentioned anything to me, but I quickly noticed that I wasn't getting invited to join client calls anymore. I decided to ask one of the employees that I had a great relationship with what was going on. He shared with me that the team didn't like it when I took over meetings, and the hallway conversation was "Don't take her on a call; she'll take over." I was so embarrassed. I had not changed my behavior from a subject matter expert to a leader. I had inadvertently created a negative brand when I thought I was adding value! As soon as I learned differently, I apologized to the individual team members I'd unintentionally impacted and told them now that I was aware, I'd be extra careful.

> **INSIGHT**
>
> A brand that serves you well in one role may not be the right brand in your next role.

After those conversations, one person took a chance and invited me to join him on a client call. Before the meeting, I visualized myself sitting in the meeting as a leader and not taking over. Before the meeting, I set an intention of not taking over, and I wrote "Don't take over" on the palm of my hand. Every time I felt like jumping in, I bit my tongue and stared at my palm. The writing on my palm reminded me to exercise my PQ—to scan my mental chatter and choose a response that was aligned with my desired branding. It was really hard for me not to jump in and take over, but I was determined to learn. In that meeting, I behaved like a leader and was very proud of myself.

Word got around that I'd changed my ways, and another person invited me to his meeting. Again, I was extra careful, and I prepared before the meeting exactly as I did for the prior meeting. I once again managed not to take over, and I added value only when needed. I congratulated and celebrated myself after the meeting.

The invitations kept coming, and I kept repeating my process. After the first few times, I found myself needing to stare at my palm less and less. After a couple of months, I didn't have to look at my palm.

I managed to change my branding from someone who takes over client calls to someone who behaves like a leader and adds value to my team's client calls.

The transition of moving from a sales expert to a leader was hard for me. It was difficult not to demonstrate the sales expertise I had worked for years to develop. However, I learned that I had to change my behavior to reflect the transition in my role to a leader. I had to intentionally build a leadership brand which also included my sales expertise.

That was just the beginning of my journey to move from my personal brand of a sales expert to a sales leader. Then, within a month of learning how to make client calls as a leader, I went for training offered by IBM for all first-time managers. When I entered the room, this was written on the whiteboard:

Treat your team the way _____.

When the class started, the instructor asked for volunteers to fill in the blank. I was the first one to raise my hand and stated, "Treat your team the way you want to be treated."

After some of the other first-time managers shared similar thoughts, the instructor filled in the correct answer on the board.

Treat your team the way <u>THEY want to be treated</u>.

Today, this is widely known as the platinum rule, but at that time, it was one of the most important leadership lessons I ever learned. It's not about me; it's about the people I lead. This moment also made me realize I needed to have a beginner's mindset as I embarked upon this new journey of leadership, so I became a sponge. I wanted to be the best leader I possibly could, and so I became a student of leadership.

First, I read leadership books (although I couldn't find any written by women). I also reflected upon every leader I'd worked with and observed the leaders around me that were respected and admired. I thought about their leadership attributes and what made them great. I also thought about what I didn't like about some leaders. I learned from my clients whom I admired as leaders. I watched how they made decisions, how they talked to their teams, how they motivated their teams, and how they solved their business problems. I looked for learning opportunities anywhere I could find them. And I kept learning and continued to improve my leadership skills until they became part of my nature. This was reflected in the impressions I left behind in all my interactions. Slowly but surely, all the newly acquired leadership attributes, combined with all my personal and unique attributes as well as my sales expertise, became my own unique leadership brand.

Later, in the Intentional Exercises section of this chapter, I'll walk you through how you can intentionally build your unique leadership brand. But first let's dive into other areas of your career where your personal branding plays a critical role.

THE IMPORTANCE OF PERSONAL BRANDING IN YOUR CURRENT ROLE

While creating a leadership brand may seem like a long-term goal, your current brand is the foundation upon which your leadership brand will be built. It's incredibly important to realize the impact your personal branding has on your career now *and* in the future. I'd like to share a story of this in action.

Every year at IBM, all first line sales leaders met with our boss to pick the winners for the Hundred Percent Club at the beginning of the year. The Hundred Percent Club recognizes the top contributors to the business for the prior year. This recognition can be an accelerator for one's career, as it was for me when I was recognized as the Rookie Systems Engineer of the Year and joined the Hundred Percent Club myself. The honor also came with world-class trips, financial rewards, and meetings with senior executives. These recognitions are what every sales representative covets and works toward the entire year.

At my first meeting, all the sales leaders came prepared to advocate for their top performers, as did I. First, we identified the outliers, those whose performances were so spectacular that no one could debate their contribution to the overall success of the business. After that, only a few slots remained, and there were many contenders, which made the competition fierce.

We all advocated for our candidates, one individual at a time—myself included. When we had only one slot left, I advocated for a woman on my team whose achievements were comparable to those of other candidates who reported to other sales leaders. As soon as I finished making a case for her, another sales leader chimed in to say that my candidate had gone out of her way to lend her expertise to someone on his team, helping the team win a critical deal that my boss needed to achieve his targets. My boss then reinforced her collaborative and helpful nature—resulting in every sales leader voting her in. She got the last slot!

In the end, what mattered was not just my advocacy for her and her performance; it was also how she was known to others in that room. The tie breaker that got her this prestigious award was what people said about her in that room: her personal brand.

Your personal branding isn't just about your performance; it's also about who you are—your personal attributes.

THE IMPORTANCE OF PERSONAL BRANDING IN YOUR JOB SEARCH

Not only is personal branding important when you're already working for an organization; it also plays a critical role in getting your ideal job. Many organizations use a technique called behavior-based interviewing to evaluate candidates, which allows the hiring managers to uncover aspects of the candidate's personal brand by asking questions that reveal the candidate's behavior in various situations.

This technique is based on the idea that people are like icebergs: The top third is what you see on their résumés in terms of knowledge, skills, and experiences. The bottom two-thirds, which aren't included on a résumé, reflect important aspects of their personal brand—their personal attributes, which often separates the stars from the superstars.

> **INSIGHT**
>
> Your personal branding isn't just about your achievements; it's also about who you are at your core.

Every job requires a certain set of competences in order for that person to thrive. For example, suppose a job requires someone who is able to navigate change with ease. Instead of directly asking about how candidates deal with change, the interviewer will evaluate their behavior by asking them to recount a situation in which they experienced a big, complex change and explain how they navigated it. Their answer to this question will reveal whether they thrive in change or not—and likely determine whether or not they get picked for the position.

And your personal brand isn't only important when you're looking for a new job outside your organization; it plays a critical role when you're looking for a position within your organization as well. I've been in conversations where the person with the most business expertise didn't get picked for a project that required significant collaboration because no one enjoyed working with her or him. The person had deep, incredible technical skills, but also had a tendency to make people feel less smart when talking to them.

THE IMPORTANCE OF PERSONAL BRANDING IN PROMOTIONS

I mentored a woman named Seema who was a first line manager, leading a team of software developers spread across the United States. She lived in Chicago, and one of her short-term definitions of success was to get promoted to the next level.

She received her first promotion not only because she was the subject matter expert on her team, but also because she outworked everyone else. She worked long hours, and her previous boss valued that. She thought the same technique would work for this promotion, so she started each day early to accommodate her team on the East Coast, and she worked late to accommodate her team on the West Coast. She checked email and responded at all hours of the day—including during dinnertime with her family and over weekends.

Eventually, an opportunity came along for promotion, and she applied. She was one of three candidates who were shortlisted for the role. The role was similar to the one she currently had, but her team would be global instead of US-based.

When she wasn't chosen for the promotion, she reached out to me. She was very upset because she thought her boss didn't value her contributions. She planned to demand an explanation from her boss and was going to start applying for jobs with other companies. Of course, if your boss doesn't appreciate the value you contribute, leaving can be the right course of action. But in this case, I knew both Seema and her boss—and I personally knew that her boss valued her contributions immensely.

I coached her to ask for feedback on what she needed to do to improve in order to better position herself for the next promotion, which is a much better approach than demanding an explanation. I told her that if her boss couldn't give her specific feedback for improvement, then she should consider leaving. But since she was happy with everything else about the company and her team, it was worth figuring out if she had a path to promotion.

She set up a meeting with her boss, who assured her that he truly valued her expertise and wanted to support her promotion. He explained that his concern was that since she was already working so many hours at her current level of responsibility, she'd be overwhelmed by leading a global team with even more people in even more time zones reporting to her. He didn't want to set her up for failure and lose her.

Seema was shocked. She thought she'd been proving her ambition and dedication by logging more hours than the rest of her team. Instead, she'd created a brand of someone who was overwhelmed at her current level of responsibility, which of course prevented her from being picked for increased responsibility. Her branding cost her a promotion, but the feedback provided insights into how her boss made decisions and what she needed to improve in order to be considered for a promotion.

During my next meeting with her, I talked to her about the importance of work-life balance and specifically about setting boundaries. As she started setting boundaries, her work-life balance improved, and as a result, she also discovered numerous other benefits:

- From her employee survey, she learned that the morale of the members of her team had improved. She'd falsely given them the impression that she expected them to work the hours she did, so many of them were also working too many hours and getting burned out.

- She improved her relationship with her husband because she wasn't constantly checking email outside of work.
- She improved her productivity and her performance.
- She sharpened her decision-making ability because she wasn't overworked.
- She enjoyed her work and her team more than ever before.

The following year, there was another promotional opportunity, and Seema got the promotion. She told me she was much more prepared to handle a global role because of my guidance on setting boundaries. She also confided in me that she was glad she didn't get the first promotion because, in her words, "I'd have been a basket case."

SUSTAINING YOUR PERSONAL BRAND

It takes many years to build a stellar personal brand, and if you don't protect it and sustain it, you could ruin it. Consistency and constant vigilance are required.

One of the key elements of sustaining your brand is recognizing when you're feeling out of sorts. All of us have situations that can get us worked up, whether it's a personal health issue, relationship issue, sick children, other sick loved ones, people undermining our capabilities, microaggressions in our workplace, or tension with coworkers. These situations can adversely impact our behavior. When this happens, become aware of how you're feeling and what's causing you to feel that way. It's OK to feel what you're feeling; what's not OK is to react when your mind is agitated and, as a result, leave negative impressions. The impressions you leave can last far beyond this moment and potentially ruin the brand you've worked so hard to build, especially if you're in the presence of people you don't frequently interact with. They could be or could become influencers or decision makers that impact your career trajectory.

Whenever you are feeling out of sorts, recognize that and pause. Scan your mental chatter and exercise your PQ to pick a response that will create or reinforce the brand you desire.

Having said that, there will also be times when you've worked so hard and diligently to build a stellar personal brand, people will be more likely to give you the benefit of the doubt when you slip for a while. For example, as I shared earlier, my team and my boss were exceptionally understanding when I was going through my personal crisis. They likely wouldn't have been so understanding if I hadn't already built a solid personal brand.

If I hadn't changed my behavior back to my original branding in a timely fashion and had missed my business performance for a few quarters in a row, a new negative personal brand would have been formed, and that would have decelerated my success. The key to sustaining your brand is to make sure your behavior, which is not aligned with your branding, is an exception and to recover as soon as you can. If your behavior doesn't change for an extended period of time, you'll start to leave less favorable impressions and form a new, less favorable brand.

CONTINUALLY IMPROVE YOUR LEADERSHIP BRAND

Even after your have created a leadership brand, as you rise higher, you must evolve as a leader, you must improve your leadership skills and learn new ones along the way. This will result in a change in your behavior, and the impressions you leave will reflect the "improved you" and form an improved leadership brand for you. Your performance will also improve as a result.

Intentionally look for opportunities to improve your leadership branding. For example, today's uncertain and ambiguous business landscape constantly creates situations beyond your control.

Everything is constantly changing. This provides the perfect opportunity to learn leadership skills to navigate uncertainty and the constantly changing business landscape. Sometimes the economy expands, and sometimes it contracts. Sometimes your business grows, and at other times it slows down or gets disrupted. No matter the specifics, view every new situation as an opportunity to learn new leadership skills and improve your existing leadership skills.

When you intentionally keep improving your leadership brand, it will help you advance into senior leadership roles. Also, your brand is how your teams will remember you long after your career is over.

A STORY OF INTENTIONAL LEADERSHIP BRANDING

Gwendolyn Sykes
Chief Financial Officer, US Secret Service

Now I'd like to share a story from a dear friend of mine who I greatly admire, Gwendolyn Sykes. Gwendolyn is the current chief financial officer (CFO) of the US Secret Service and previous CFO of NASA, Yale University, and Morehouse College. She's worked with some of our country's most prestigious organizations, and each has hired her not just for her ability to get the job done, but also because of her stellar leadership brand, which includes trust and integrity. The story she shares illustrates the power of your brand to move you ahead in your career. It also shows how your brand follows you across companies, industries, and over time.

It's not just what people in your organization say about you that matters when it comes to your brand, but also how you're known by others outside your organization. Her story also shows how, when you're driven by trust and integrity, it gives

you the confidence to stand up to anyone to protect your brand, regardless of how high up the person is in the organization.

Every story has a beginning, and mine began in Anchorage, Alaska, in a small town in the early 1970s. My parents moved there when I was 10 or 11 years old, because my dad was in the military. Trust and integrity were the cornerstone of my family upbringing, and as I grew up, I had many life experiences that taught me never to compromise on those two key elements.

As a young adult at 16, I had the great opportunity to work for Senator Ted Stevens as a high school intern. I was going to Washington, DC, to see how the government really works. I learned a lot from him about how to be a true public servant, with integrity. His ability to win reelections was significantly based on the trust of Alaskans.

Unfortunately, he lost his senatorship, but he's rewritten the prosecutorial misconduct book for all law books, because his case, which I was a part of, is the grandest case of prose-cutorial misconduct. I was a personal representative for him, so I had a personal conversation about what I thought about his integrity. I had to put my brand on trial with him. I believed in what I was standing for, and I stood up for him—I trusted him. I believed in his integrity. He was convicted.

Upon further investigation, it was found that the prosecu-tion withheld a key witness statement that would have com-pletely exonerated the senator as well as stopped the trial/case. In the end, the case was overturned, but the false con-viction lost him the election. I can still clearly remember him saying, "Where does a man go to get his integrity back?" That moment has stuck with me throughout my career and my life.

I know deep down that integrity is key, and my experience with Senator Stevens cements that belief. Integrity can never be for sale. If you get that little funny feeling in your gut, don't do it. If it doesn't feel right, don't sell your soul. That's the brand of Gwendolyn Sykes: high integrity. One thing that I tell all my staff—from NASA to Yale to the Secret Service—is "You work for Gwendolyn Sykes. And Gwendolyn Sykes says, 'If someone's pressuring you to do something and it doesn't seem right, step back and don't do it.' Because if you do something wrong, it impacts not only your credibility, but my credibility, also."

Before I began to work at NASA, I was in the Pentagon, working in Program and Financial Control, helping manage a budget of billions of dollars.

I remember a time when I was in my mid-thirties, I went to a meeting with a brigadier general. He was wearing his army uniform with all its stars, and his accounting team was telling him one thing, my budget team was pointing out inconsistencies telling me another, and I was to come to a consensus on how we could work together. And this gentleman smacked his hand down on the table and said, "I don't really care, young lady, what you're coming in for. We're gonna do it this way."

I politely pushed back my chair, and I smacked my hand down on the table right back and said, "Sir, while you may lead this office, you're being led down a path, and it is not the right path. And I'm here to tell you why." Then I asked to clear the room and have a conversation, "so we can," I said, "keep moving in the right direction."

He took a deep breath and ordered that the room be cleared. And then I walked him through all the issues.

My branding of trust and integrity gave me the confidence to stand my ground, and it was displayed in full force during our conversation. And to this day, we're still best friends.

While I was working in the Pentagon, I was pursued for the position of CFO of NASA because of my branding. I accepted, and in this new position, everyone's trust in me enabled us to solve what seemed like unsolvable problems. We succeeded in changing the financial system, which previous teams had tried to change five times prior to my onboarding. My branding of trust and integrity enabled me to earn the respect and confidence of everyone in the NASA organization, including the most skeptical people, the scientists.

At NASA, I served as a presidential appointee. So when Bush was no longer president, I landed a job as Yale University's first CFO.

During my time in that position, my mother was diagnosed with breast cancer and my father with dementia, which developed into full-blown Alzheimer's. I knew I couldn't keep up with the demands of my position at Yale and take care of my parents, who lived in Atlanta. So I prioritized my parents and decided to move to Atlanta. Reverend Doctor Franklin, the president of Morehouse College, heard this news and called me. He said, "I heard you're leaving Yale. Would you be interested in joining us at Morehouse College?" I explained my situation, and he said the college could provide me with cultural and family support. I know that my branding of trust and integrity played a significant role.

He and the college did a fabulous job. I was able to fully support my parents through that time period, and I was able to stop working 30 days before my father passed away so I could be with him in his final days.

I began where I ended: My dad began my journey, my dad was with me through the end, and he's still with me. Find that balance between personal and professional as you go through your life's journey, because that also becomes part of your personal branding.

INTENTIONAL EXERCISES

Now it's time to create and execute your strategy of Intentional Leadership Branding. Let's start with Introspection, so you can gain knowledge of your current personal brand and your desired leadership brand. Then we'll move to the Application section, so you can apply the insights you learned in this chapter and intentionally start building your leadership brand. We'll wrap things up with Reflection and Celebration to look back, course-correct, and celebrate your successes of moving toward the brand you desire.

Even though your personal branding is about how you're known in terms of both your personal attributes and your business expertise, for the purpose of this exercise, we'll focus on your personal attributes rather than business expertise. Building your business expertise is critical for your performance, but for leadership roles where the competition is fierce, each candidate competing for the role will have the business expertise. It's your unique and authentic personal attributes that will be your differentiators.

So let's get started!

Introspection

This exercise is broken into two parts:

1. Your current personal brand
2. Your desired leadership brand

Your Current Personal Brand

Answer the following questions:

- What are my top ten best personal attributes that contribute toward my success?
- Do I consistently leave impressions that demonstrate those attributes?
- Do people seek me out for those attributes?
- Which of those attributes make me unique?
- When was the last time I left an impression that was not aligned with my best personal attributes?
- When I am feeling out of sorts, how do I behave?
- Do I have people who care enough to tell me what others are talking about me?

Your Desired Leadership Brand

Let's discover the leadership attributes you want to acquire that will help you become the leader you want to become and help you achieve your long-term definition of success. Answer the following questions:

- What are the personal attributes of the leaders I respect and admire who are in the role I want in five years?
- What leadership traits do I admire the most about the leaders I've worked for in the past?
- What leadership qualities does my company look for in its leaders?
- Which leadership qualities do organizations that I aspire to work for look for when hiring leaders?

- What are the attributes of a leader I want to work for?
- Ten years from now, how do I want to be remembered by the people who work for me?

Your answers are the desired leadership traits you'll intentionally acquire.

IMPORTANT LEADERSHIP ATTRIBUTES

If you're not sure where to get started with your list of leadership attributes, here are some suggestions:

- **Be trustworthy and respectful.** Building trust and respect must be the foundation of your leadership brand. Keep in mind that you can't build trust by pretending to be someone else. You must be authentic and transparent, with actions that reflect sincere intentions. Treat everyone with dignity and respect.
- **Be caring.** Leadership is about how you guide your team. Build a reputation as someone who genuinely cares about the members of her team and wants them to succeed. Express genuine care and concern, and have their backs when they're facing difficult situations. Find opportunities for your team to shine, praise the team's successes often, and share credit generously.
- **Practice effective listening.** Being able to listen effectively is a very important leadership skill. When people feel heard, they will voice their opinions and they're more loyal to you because you showed them respect and regard. Effective listening also gives you knowledge and perspectives that increase your leadership capacity.

- **Communicate clearly.** Communicating with clarity and conviction is a required leadership skill, especially when you need to handle conflicts between the team members, and encourage people to work together. It's also necessary to promote your vision and persuade others to buy into it. Build a brand of being an effective communicator when times are great as well as when times are tough.
- **Inspire optimism.** Leaders who are optimists have an infectious can-do attitude. They have a sense of purpose and envision a better future. They're able to inspire and motivate people to work toward achieving a shared vision of success. They focus on what can go right and don't wallow in what can go wrong.
- **Be intellectually curious.** The best leaders are intellectually curious. They're hungry to learn more and understand the other person's point of view. This leads to better decision-making and problem-solving. It also makes your team feel included and respected.
- **Advocate for inclusion.** Inclusive leaders set the tone and model the behaviors that create an environment where the individual members feel they belong; are understood, appreciated, valued, and respected; and are able to contribute at their maximum capacity. Inclusive leaders invite diverse perspectives to deliver spectacular business results.
- **Nurture potential.** The best leaders look for opportunities to help everyone on their team grow so they can realize their maximum potential. They give individuals added responsibilities and hold them accountable while also being their coach when needed. These leaders build people up during setbacks and energize them to keep moving forward.

- **Face adversity and crisis.** The best leaders are those who can face adverse situations (which are inevitable) with dignity and magnanimity. They accept responsibility and don't blame their team when things don't go perfectly according to plan. These leaders work with their team to come up with innovative and creative solutions. They convey difficult messages well, and when the environment gets chaotic and the road ahead isn't clear, they use discerning judgment to transform chaos into clarity.
- **Create success no matter the circumstances.** In today's disrupted world, leaders don't control the factors that influence their success, but they do control the outcomes. They don't wait for circumstances to change; they pivot and figure out a way to succeed no matter what the circumstances.

Application

Start by adding "Intentional Leadership Branding" as a priority in your PSP. This will serve as a weekly reminder to become intentional about the impressions you're leaving in all your interactions.

At this point you'll have defined what success means to you; you're allocating your attention to the tasks, meetings, and activities that will give you the best chance of achieving your success; you're setting an intention every day to create value at your maximum capacity in all your interactions; and you're setting an intention every day to grow at your maximum capacity in all those interactions. You are also building and sustaining meaningful relationships every day. Now, let's turn our attention to the impressions you leave behind in all your interactions. These impressions will form your personal brand.

How can you intentionally build a leadership brand?

In order to intentionally build a leadership brand, first and foremost, before you begin your workday, meeting, conversation, or new experience, set an intention to leave impressions that reflect the leadership brand you desire. When you know who you are, who you want to become, and how you want to be known, it becomes an internal compass that drives your behavior. You will become vigilant about the impressions you leave behind no matter what the circumstances. You will take the necessary steps to become the leader that deserves that leadership brand.

The following steps will help you build your unique leadership brand:

1. Determine your unique intentional leadership brand by combining your current personal brand (which consists of your current business expertise and personal attributes) and the desired leadership traits you identified in the Introspection section.

2. Reinforce your current personal brand by intentionally leaving impressions that demonstrate your business expertise as well as your top personal attributes in all your interactions. Pay special attention to demonstrate your unique attributes. In today's busy workplace, if you are not intentional about the impressions you leave behind, you could potentially leave behind less favorable impressions on autopilot by rushing through a meeting or not being fully engaged.

    When you experience biases or micro-aggressions in the workplace, recognize that you are feeling out of sorts. Pause and scan your mental chatter to choose a response that will reinforce your brand and keep you moving towards your definitions of success. Don't react to anyone else's behavior—otherwise you will give your power to them and also ruin your personal brand you worked so hard to build.

3. Start adding leadership attributes to your brand by acquiring one or two leadership attributes at a time.

From the list of leadership attributes you want to acquire, pick one or two that you believe will be easiest for you to master, and get to work. Only focusing on one or two attributes at once allows you to experience success right away, motivates you to keep going, and prepares you to acquire the more difficult traits.

I have to point out that when I say "easiest," I don't mean this will be easy. I just mean that this trait is one you'll be able to make a part of your brand quicker than others. The reality is, you should expect this to be hard work. You're changing from the inside, so be patient and persistent. As you learn and improve upon these leadership skills, you'll become proficient, and then it will be time to take on your next one or two skills you want to acquire.

Let me walk you through a simple example of how you can acquire a leadership attribute you don't currently possess. Let's say effective listening is the critical leadership skill you want to possess. With this in mind, here are five things you can do right now to change your leadership brand to include the attribute of an effective listener:

1. Learn about becoming an effective listener by reading books or observing effective listeners—whatever way you learn best.
2. Set an intention to "listen effectively" every day when you go to work as well as every time you enter a meeting.
3. Write on your palm "listen" as a reminder, especially when going into meetings in which you have a tendency to interrupt.
4. Let a few of your trusted colleagues know that you want to become an effective listener and need their help. Every time you interrupt someone, ask your "designated" colleagues to call you out. Get your family and friends involved, and ask them to do the same!

5. When possible, create a tangible consequence like putting money in a jar or buying lunch or dinner for the person you interrupted.
6. Seek feedback from your trusted folks about what people are saying about you.

No matter which leadership trait you want to acquire, you can do little things each day to improve that particular skill. As you start applying these tactics, you'll notice slow and steady progress. That's not to say you won't slip once in a while, because you will. But it's important to recover as quickly as possible and keep at it until you master the trait. Persistency and consistency are key to learning a new personal trait.

Once you master a leadership trait, intentionally look for opportunities to demonstrate that trait in the impressions you leave behind— slowly but surely you'll become known for it, and it will become part of your leadership branding. Once you've mastered one leadership attribute, move to the next and do this process again and again.

While you may not have a leadership brand currently, the exciting news is that the work you're doing now will ensure you're viewed as a leader, setting you up to get promoted into a leadership role—and be successful once you get there. Your leadership brand plays a critical role in helping you achieve your definitions of success—both short- and long-term.

Intentionally keep evolving as a leader and improving your leadership brand. This work never ends as you can always become a better and better leader.

Reflection and Celebration

During your weekly reflection time, ask yourself the following questions:

- When did I leave impressions that are aligned with my leadership brand?

- When did I leave impressions that aren't aligned with my leadership brand?
- What do I need to do next week to course-correct?

Based on the answer to the second question, course-correct without beating yourself up. You can't belittle yourself to greatness. It's important to focus on progress and not on perfection. This is hard work, so be kind and patient with yourself. If you need a reminder, set a calendar reminder to intentionally leave impressions of your intended leadership brand. This will ensure you don't fall back to autopilot.

No matter what, congratulate yourself for your answer to the first question, because that *is* progress you made toward building your leadership brand. Reflect upon this answer, be grateful for the opportunities you were presented with this week to build and reinforce your leadership brand, and celebrate yourself for making progress. This process will motivate you to make more progress the following week.

Over time, intentionally keep learning more and more leadership attributes, which will be reflected in the impressions you leave behind and will form your desired leadership brand. Your leadership brand will be reflected in how you are known.

SET YOUR INTENTIONS

Promise yourself:
- I will become intentional about leaving impressions that are aligned with my desired leadership brand.
- I will always protect my brand and never compromise it.
- I will keep growing into the person I want to become and the leader I was meant to be by intentionally building and improving my leadership brand.

8

INTENTIONAL
PROMOTION

*Women belong in all places where
decisions are being made. It shouldn't be
that women are the exception.*
Ruth Bader Ginsburg

The eighth and final strategy that will help you emerge as a leader
is Intentional Promotion. As you execute and master the first seven
strategies, you'll gain a deep knowledge of your worth and show your
worth in all your interactions and your achievements—proving you're
ready to get a promotion to a leadership role.

That doesn't mean that you'll be handed a promotion. You must
become intentional about positioning yourself for consideration,
asking for and getting your well-deserved promotion with discipline, stubborn determination, and a game plan, which is the focus
of this chapter.

On top of the traditional obstacles that come with promotion to a
leadership level, women have many added layers to deal with. The first

one being: In most organizations, because there aren't enough women, and especially women of color, visible in leadership roles, decision makers and influencers have a hard time envisioning us as leaders.

Also, getting a promotion is a process that requires you to advocate for yourself as the best possible candidate for the role, but the reality is that many of us aren't comfortable doing this for ourselves. We prefer to wait for others to recognize our capabilities and potential and promote us. If that worked, the number of women in leadership roles and especially senior leadership roles wouldn't be as dire as it is.

Another problem we face is that because we don't see enough women in leadership roles, many women get discouraged and give up on themselves before they realize their leadership potential. You are reading this book because you aspire to become a leader. So right now I want you to make a commitment to yourself that you'll give it all you've got to get promoted into a leadership position and then continue to reach senior leadership positions. Commit that you'll never give up on yourself, because when you know you're destined to become a leader not only will you realize your leadership potential, but you will also become part of the change that creates gender parity in leadership roles. And when there's gender parity in leadership roles, we'll be present in every room where decisions are being made—diminishing negative stereotypes and biases in the workplace once and for all. Your promotion into a leadership role is not just for you but also for all the other women who will come after you. You are blazing a trail for them.

Our world needs women like you who aspire to emerge as leaders. We have unique perspectives, compassionate viewpoints, and ingenious ideas that can bring about positive change. The good news is that business leaders are waking up to this fact that women leaders are necessary for their success. Many have realized the advantages of having women in leadership roles to deliver better business results. Many are changing their policies to ensure they can attract, retain, and promote women. Now is the time for you to seize this opportunity by showing your worth and getting promoted into a leadership role.

———

There's no magic formula for when you will get your first promotion. Some women believe that if they don't get their first promotion by the age of 30, they've lost the opportunity to emerge as a leader. And still others believe they can't be a mother and a leader at work. I can tell you, none of this is true—from my own experience and the experiences of all the women I've worked with. In fact, I started my career at 25, and it took me over 10 years before I got my first promotion. I had just turned 36. My daughter, Sophia, was almost 4 years old, and my son, Samir, was 2. My second promotion was in two years after my first.

Be aware that these and any other self-limiting beliefs diminish your chances of promotion. Remember from our work so far that your beliefs will prove themselves right, so watch your mental chatter closely and use your PQ to create a strong belief that you deserve to and will get promoted into leadership roles. I did, and that's the only reason I reached the levels I did in my career.

Let me share with you how I got my first promotion to a leadership role.

As you read in Chapter 1, once I started excelling in sales at IBM, I knew I'd found the perfect role in which I could excel and advance my career. This inspired me to define my long-term success to become a sales leader in five years.

In my fourth year, my son, Samir, was born. Sophia was 2½ years old at the time, and my husband and I wanted our children to grow up around extended family just as we both had. Our parents were, respectively, in Tanzania and India. Since our next closest relatives were in

Vancouver, British Columbia, we decided to move from Minneapolis to Seattle to be closer to them.

At the time, the only opening in the Seattle office was for a sales representative whose job was to sell to clients of our competitors. Since these clients had no previous working relationship with IBM and had working relationships with our competitors, selling to them was incredibly difficult, and the chance of winning deals was very slim. Most people didn't want to take on that job, and my hiring manager, Sandy, said as much. I figured that my sales expertise would help me navigate this challenge, and if I succeeded in this role, I would move faster toward my longer-term vision of success. I accepted the job and the challenge.

And it was a challenge. Even after four months, most clients didn't even want to meet with me, and the ones that did weren't welcoming. Some talked to me just so they could show their bosses that they'd considered multiple options, and others made up their minds before they even met me. Even though I knew I was being used by them, I continued to compete for their business. I received rejection after rejection, and I didn't close a single deal in the first five months on the job. After so many frustrating moments and days, I wasn't sure if I could succeed, but I framed every loss and rejection as a learning opportunity to try and win the next deal.

Eventually my inherent resilience, stubborn determination to succeed, and perseverance paid off. I finally won my first deal—and it happened to be a multimillion-dollar deal that became a turning point in my career.

While winning this deal was the hardest thing I'd done in my entire career, it was also the most fulfilling. (In many cases, they seem to go hand in hand.) This deal earned me multiple very prestigious awards and recognitions. And while I was incredibly proud of the fact that I felt like I made the impossible possible, I knew I couldn't have won this deal without the support of many other people who helped me. I made sure their managers knew they were instrumental in helping me win the deal. I also recognized them while receiving my awards. This helped me build great relationships with my new team.

I monitored the delivery of our solution every step of the way, from start to finish. I anticipated and fixed challenges before the client even noticed. My client was so pleased with me that he offered to be a reference for my future prospects.

Winning this "impossible deal" gave me a great deal of visibility and boosted my competence and confidence exponentially. It energized me to pursue more challenging deals. And now I had enthusiastic support from so many people who had supported me in my first deal and, most importantly, a reference from a client. I started winning more impressive deals.

These wins almost always required the approval and support of my boss as well as of many other senior executives because I had to structure deals that were outside the norm. As I pursued and won more of these unique and challenging deals, I gained more and more visibility. I built solid working relationships with my boss, his boss, and many other senior executives, including Rodney Adkins, who was the general manager of our hardware business and five levels higher than my boss. When he visited Seattle, I took him on client calls with me, and he witnessed my achievements firsthand, including my ability to win the trust and confidence of some of the toughest clients. This set the foundation for Rod to become my sponsor eight years later.

> **INSIGHT**
>
> The easiest way to get visibility is to do what everyone else thinks is impossible.

Winning these deals gave me an opportunity to learn and demonstrate many leadership skills in ways my previous role did not. My boss, as well as my line of management, had a front row seat to watch me demonstrate my leadership skills.

In the following three months, I won three other deals, which enabled me to make my entire year's revenue target, and each earned me more accolades.

Since my performance was so spectacular, for the first time in my 11-year career I felt that I deserved to get promoted. I decided it was the perfect time to initiate a conversation for getting promoted.

I set up a meeting with my boss and expressed my desire to get promoted to a sales leader. By his body language and a supportive facial expression, I found him to be supportive of my desire. I asked the following four questions:

1. What do I need to demonstrate in order to be considered for the position?
2. Are there any gaps in my skills that I need to fill?
3. What were his decision-making criteria?
4. What was the decision-making process?

He told me to keep performing the way I had for the past five months and that there were no gaps I needed to fill. He complimented my performance and the leadership skills I demonstrated to win multiple new clients. He shared his decision-making criteria as well as the decision-making process.

With his agreement, I also met with his boss, who agreed with my boss's perspective. And I talked to my mentor at the time, Susan Whitney, and asked her for guidance on how I could ensure I was the best possible candidate when the job was available. She advised me to ensure my performance kept exceeding everyone's expectations and to behave as if I were already a sales leader. I did just that.

> **INSIGHT**
>
> Engaging senior executives in your projects gives you visibility.

At the end of the year, I exceeded every business objective and continued to demonstrate my leadership skills, enabling me to meet all the decision-making criteria. I knew I'd be highly rated, so during my performance appraisal, I asked if I could be considered to compete for the position of a sales leader. My boss agreed.

Eight months later, there was an opening for a sales leader for which I got an opportunity to compete, and I got promoted to a sales leader. I achieved my long-term definition of success!

Another dream came true for me that day, and I was deeply grateful for this golden opportunity of leadership. I reflected upon my journey and was in awe of this defining moment of my career. I was once a young girl whose toys, as noted earlier in the book, were kitchen utensils and soda bottles in Tanzania, and now I was a sales leader with 10 people reporting to me and a sales target of $120 million at one of the most admired technology companies in the world. There were no other sales leaders who looked like me. I was overwhelmed with success and gratitude. I took time to soak in my success and internalized everything I had accomplished. I celebrated with my family, went on a spa retreat, and thanked every person who had helped me in any way on my journey to leadership. I felt successful in every ounce of my being, which energized me to do everything in my power to become an exemplary sales leader and keep pursuing even more success.

After my first promotion, the eight intentional strategies continued to help me rise higher and higher, until I became a vice president—one of the highest-ranking women of color at IBM. Many of these strategies continue to help me to this day. For example, as I am writing this book, I am intentional about creating maximum value for you.

As I rose up the leadership ladder, I gained deeper insights into how promotions work. While every company, every role, and every promotion are different, there are a few universal principles that will increase your chances of getting promoted. These principles have helped me and many other women get promotions, and I'm excited to share them with you now to make your promotion a reality!

THREE PREREQUISITES TO GET A PROMOTION

Before you even begin the process of asking for a promotion, there are three prerequisites you must fulfill.

1. Know That You Deserve to Get Promoted

Your promotion, like most other things in life, starts with the right mindset. You must start with the belief that you deserve to get promoted. Only with that mindset will you be able to take the necessary steps required to get promoted.

Don't let any self-limiting beliefs or naysayers create any doubts in your mind. All the self-knowledge you have gained by working through the exercises in this book will keep you grounded and make you comfortable in your own skin—this helps you to not be influenced negatively by anyone else. Focus on what you know and what you can learn as opposed to what you don't know or haven't learned. Many of us are wired to give more attention to what we don't know, and you must change that. Always remember that there is not a single person on the face of this earth that knows everything, and there are always going to be opportunities to learn more than you know right now.

2. Make Sure an Opportunity Exists

In order for a promotion to occur, opportunity has to meet preparation. Regardless of how prepared you are, if there's no opportunity for promotion, you won't get promoted. Many women get stuck in careers with short ladders. Never allow yourself to be stuck in a position or an organization that doesn't have promotional opportunities for you. You must go where the opportunities exists. The more growth your business is experiencing, the more opportunities there'll be for you to get promoted.

3. Acknowledge and Embrace Pivots

For women, we have an added layer of complexity: life situations that require us to acknowledge and embrace pivots in order to get promoted, and I'm no exception to this.

In 2008, I faced the difficult decision of leaving IBM because the next step in my career would require me to move away from Seattle. This wasn't an option for me at the time because my children were in high school and I wasn't willing to relocate. I spoke with my mentors and sponsors, and we all agreed that leaving the company was the best decision for me. I accepted the position of senior vice president of sales at a medium-sized technology company, but it didn't work out; six months after that, I started my own company as an IBM business partner. The financial crisis hit a few months later, and in the middle of shutting my business down, I received a call from Rod Adkins asking if I'd be interested in interviewing for a vice president–level position that had just opened up at IBM and was the perfect fit for me. In October 2011, I went back to IBM with title of Vice President of the IBM/Microsoft Global Alliance.

As my story demonstrates, promotions don't always happen linearly or as you plan them, so be prepared to embrace the situation and pivot when those inevitable detours come your way. Also, remember that no decision is final. If one decision doesn't work, find another that does, and keep moving toward more senior levels of leadership.

Setbacks and detours don't mean you can't get back on the leadership pipeline. Don't give up on your dreams, pivot and get back on track. Reframe your thinking and recognize that pivots like this can provide an opportunity to expand your skills and improve your chances for future success.

FOUR STEPS TO BECOMING THE BEST CANDIDATE FOR PROMOTION

Become the best possible candidate for a promotion by following these four steps:

1. Master the First Seven Strategies

A promotion isn't a one-time event. Consider each day on your job as an interview for your next promotion. Diligently and persistently execute the strategies in this book on a daily basis.

As you master all the strategies we've worked through together, you become a stronger contender for the promotion. Think of every strategy as an interdependent link in a chain. The more you master each strategy, the stronger the links become. Some strategies may be harder to master than others and will take more time and patience, and that's OK. You must persist and never give up.

2. Demonstrate Leadership Skills

By building a leadership brand, the people you interact with on a daily basis will already view you as a leader, but you must ensure that your boss and other decision makers see your leadership abilities, too. If your current position doesn't offer you opportunities to demonstrate leadership, look for situations that do, such as taking the initiative to lead a task force or tackling any other project for your boss that gives your boss and many other decision makers and influencers a front row seat to witness your leadership capabilities. An added bonus is to take on additional responsibility in your current position so you can start operating at the scope of a leader even before getting promoted.

Another bonus is to gain visibility of your leadership capabilities at the senior executive level.

3. Share Your Leadership Ambition

Share your ambition to become a leader openly and widely. Share it with your peers, anyone else you've formed a relationship with in your line of management, and any senior executives you engage with. Everyone should know you're ambitious and are working hard to get promoted to a leadership position. One part of your personal brand should be "She's ambitious." When others know you have leadership ambitions, they might help you.

4. Engage Your Mentors and Others

Make a list of all the people you believe can help you get promoted. This can include (previous or current) bosses, mentors, sponsors, and other connections who are decision makers that promote leaders in your organization.

Narrow this down to the top three to five people you believe can help you the most to get promoted, and set up meetings with each with the objective to:

- Ask what you need to demonstrate to be picked for the role.
- Ask how they got their promotion.
- Ask what leadership attributes helped them the most once they were in that role.

Listen, learn, and implement their guidance to make yourself the best possible candidate.

A STORY OF
INTENTIONAL PROMOTION

Erica Qualls-Battey
Marriott's Area General Manager in Atlanta

My friend Erica Qualls-Battey is Marriott's area general manager in Atlanta—one of Marriott's largest markets. As a Black woman who started with a part-time job answering phones, she's already received 16 promotions. Here's her remarkable story, which illustrates the importance of letting others know what you want moving up, and being open to new experiences for learning, growing, and exceeding expectations. She's also a great example of using doubters to motivate her. The most important takeaway is how she used her influence to have discussions with her CEO to make a difference for other women coming after her.

I was born in Philadelphia. My mom and dad divorced when I was eight, and I'm the youngest of five children. My mom instilled in us a strong sense of responsibility for family and community at an early age. She was loving, kind, and determined, and most importantly, she was fearless. In 1979, after attending a Marvin Gaye concert in San Francisco, she decided to raise her children in California. She sold her bakery and her home and packed up her five children and moved us to San Jose, because she said her children were going to have a better life than what Philadelphia offered.

My mother taught us that education was critical, as well as self-awareness, strength, and compassion for others. She'd take in any people who needed her, she'd feed them and their families, and she made it known that *we had to give more than we thought we should receive*. She also had this profound understanding that the lens through which the world would evaluate our performance is sharper and longer than the lens used to assess others.

As I grew into the adult woman I am today, I decided I was going to choose to be the best wife, mother, and business-woman I could be, *not only to create my own legacy but to carry on her legacy.* And that was important to me. My mom was determined that her children would be successful, and that we'd rely on God and ourselves to make it in the world.

My original goal was to help young adults, but I learned that the problem was much bigger than me. So I decided I'd raise my own kids, give them the world, and see how that worked out.

I joined the hotel industry after my husband and I had our fourth child. We still lived in San Jose, which has an extremely high cost of living. I shared with a friend that I wanted a part-time job, just Friday and Saturday nights. She shared that the Santa Clara Marriott was hiring a PBX operator, answering phones. So I said I'd take it.

At that point I was a stay-at-home mom to four kids. When you're in that position, it's very normal to need a break. And that's what the work at Marriott was supposed to be. Two nights a week answering phones and having fun. What I learned was that it was dynamic and fast-paced. The environ-ment was great, and the core values of the company aligned with my own. Over the next 28 years, I went on to work in finance, operations, human resources, and sales at Marriott. I've been promoted 16 times.

When people ask about my journey, I always talk about the importance of moving quickly and not letting dust get underneath your feet. When you're in this industry, *you can learn an awful lot, and you can move up quickly.*

I knew after the first few months that I wanted to build a career at Marriott International, because it's a people-first company. Within three months, I went from being a part-time phone operator to a full-time night auditor. I told everyone who'd listen that I was going to be the vice president of operations.

I always tell my mentees, *when you know the position you want, let others know, because you never know who'll be a sponsor for you.* A person might be in a room and hear of an opportunity and say, "I know someone looking for that." Or someone might connect you with a person who's in the position you want—which is exactly what happened to me.

People are fearful of being turned down, so they don't say what they want, but you have to tell people, and you have to show that you have the skills and you're gonna go for it.

As I mentioned above, I was telling people that I wanted to be vice president of operations. When the vice president of operations came to the hotel, my general manager told him, "I want you to meet someone." My general manager set up a time for us to speak, and I asked the vice president of operations to tell me about his job.

He said, "Well, I travel four out of five days a week," and in that moment, I realized I needed a new dream job, because as a mother of four, that wouldn't be it. But I knew I still wanted to be the highest-ranking person in the building. Then I started thinking, I wanted to be a general manager of a really large, beautiful hotel. And as a general manager, there's a lot to understand about the business. So I started thinking, "How do I learn?"

I used the resources that were available to me. I took extra classes, and I signed up for everything. I also made sure I learned the metrics that mattered to our company: guest satisfaction, revenue, profitability, owner relations, employee engagement. I wanted to learn the business: What does a successful hotel look like? And then I took on those jobs. Whenever a job opened, I applied for it. I also talked to mentors and friends, and I *always looked for ways to improve a process.*

I thought that becoming general manager was a five- to ten-year plan, but it ended up being a much shorter time frame. It was about four years.

The general manager at the time saw something great in me, because I always signed up for meaningful assignments and because I'd take on anything. I was in a meeting, and he asked me if I'd consider going to Residence Inn, which is our extended-stay brand. And I said yes without even knowing what that would mean, because he said, "You go to this branch, and you'll be a general manager in a year."

I came to the Residence Inn as assistant general manager, and within a year, the general manager was promoted, and I took her place. The property was struggling. There were issues with finance and with theft. And *challenges like that created opportunities for spectacular performance.* We turned that Residence Inn around and made it the number one revenue maker in the United States.

My next move was to Atlanta as director of human resources. Now, you may ask why I'd leave Residence Inn, where I had the top job of general manager, to go to Atlanta, where I would take a lesser job as director of human resources. Atlanta was better both from a family perspective and for my career. I was going from a 478-room building to a 1,600-room hotel with 1,200 people working there, so it was a much larger hotel with much bigger revenues, and now I was an executive committee member. Because, remember, I still had a goal of being a general manager of a large, beautiful hotel. And *sometimes reaching your goal in a strategic, intentional way means taking one step backward to get to take two steps forward.*

While working in the human resources department, our employee engagement scores were very low, so there was a ton of opportunity for improvement. We worked tirelessly to improve before I moved on to a hotel manager role. Three years later, my general manager informed me that he was leaving the Atlanta Marriott Marquis and wanted me to apply for his role. I didn't know if the decision makers would accept someone who was previously a general manager of a property as small as the Residence Inn, but I didn't let that stop me.

And when I got the job, everyone asked me how I got it. And the answer is this: *Understanding what metrics matter, going after where the opportunities are, making a difference, helping your team along, and driving your business in a phenomenal way can lead to really fabulous things.* Delivering is just the baseline: You have to exceed. And I keep saying that, because I think people believe if they keep their head down and they work really hard, they're going to get noticed. *The reality is, you get noticed by making a difference.* Find one thing that really matters and become an expert at that. Benchmark against the best, and fight to exceed that number. And all the while, have fun at what you're doing! Confucius is reputed to have said, "Find a job you enjoy doing, and you will never have to work a day in your life." And that's what I did when I joined Marriott.

There were naysayers. Someone told me, "There are no general managers who look like you. There are no women general managers, and you're a Black woman." And I never forgot that. When I became general manager of the Atlanta Marriott Marquis, which is Marriott's third-largest hotel, I called that person, who was also on the path to be a general manager, just to let him know. He was blown away.

When he told me, "You don't fit the profile or the look," that created a fire in my belly. It became a motivator. I had something unique to offer the company. My skills, talents, and abilities were just what Marriott needed.

If I'm not creating breadth and depth for the next legacy, then I'm not creating value. Marriott International, as well as other companies throughout the world, needs that fire to create a world that includes everyone—and to create meaningful lives.

Arne Sorenson, our late CEO, was a person who never came in with a bunch of answers; he always asked questions: "Are we doing the right things?" "What should we change?" If we created new processes, he would get opinions from across the corporation.

When I shared information about diversity and inclusion with Arne, he would ask if the numbers mattered or if the individual people mattered. And I said: "Arne, until people can look up and see more than one senior leader of color, more than one senior leader who's a woman, the numbers matter. The numbers matter because they say to individuals climbing the ranks, 'There's room for me.'"

> And today we have so many more senior-ranking women. I think it's important that you have to state what you see and share it with senior leaders.

INTENTIONAL EXERCISES

Now it's time to create and execute your strategy of Intentional Promotion. These exercises will be relevant once you have become the best possible candidate for a promotion. Depending on how far you are from getting your promotion, you might not be able to answer all the questions. Go through it once and answer what you can and then come back to this chapter and exercises when you're ready to get promoted. It's always good to begin with the end in mind.

Let's start with Introspection, so you can gain knowledge of where you currently are in the process of getting your promotion. Then we'll move to the Application section, so you can apply the insights you learned in this chapter and intentionally start positioning yourself for your promotion and work toward getting promoted.

Introspection

Let's do some introspection to determine where you currently are in the process of getting your promotion. Ask yourself these questions:

The Prerequisites for Getting a Promotion
- Do I believe I can get promoted?
- Does an opportunity exist for the promotion I'm seeking in my organization?

- Do I have any personal situations I need to embrace and pivot to ensure I remain in the leadership pipeline?

Becoming the Best Possible Candidate

- Am I intentionally allocating my attention to my highest priorities every day?
- Am I contributing value at my maximum capacity every day?
- Am I contributing to the success of my boss outside my job responsibilities?
- Am I contributing to the success of my organization?
- Am I growing at my maximum capacity every day?
- Have I demonstrated my growth potential?
- Am I able to prioritize the demands of my work and my personal life?
- Have I created a leadership brand?
- How is my relationship with my boss?
- How does my boss get to witness my leadership potential?
- Do my mentors know I want to get promoted?
- Do I have mentors or other connections that can help me become the best possible candidate?
- Have I shared my leadership ambitions widely?
- If I'm competing for an executive position or I'm one of the few exceptional candidates competing for the promotion, do I have a sponsor who'll advocate for me?
- What were my last two performance ratings?
- Am I one of the highest-ranked members of my team?
- Am I on my organization's top talent list?
- What awards and recognitions have I won in the past two years?

Promotion Readiness

- When do I plan on having an initial conversation with my boss about my desire to get promoted?
- Do I know the promotion process in my organization?
- Am I comfortable advocating for myself?
- What's my plan to become the best possible candidate?
- When will I become the best possible candidate?
- Do I know who'll be the decision makers and influencers for the promotion I'll seek?
- How do I plan to engage my mentors and sponsors to help me get promoted?

Application

Once you've done the work to become the best possible candidate, you're ready to initiate the process of being promoted to a leadership position—with people reporting to you and wider responsibilities. Do this by first, adding "Intentional Promotion" to your priorities in your PSP. This will serve as a weekly reminder of the fact that you are in the process of getting your leadership role. Granted that promotions work differently for every organization, every level of leadership, and every boss, the following steps will make your promotion a reality.

First and foremost, you must internalize the fact that you are the best candidate for the role so you can advocate for yourself. Many of us aren't comfortable advocating for ourselves, and we must change that. If you can't advocate for yourself, you can't expect anyone else to advocate for you.

If you are not comfortable advocating for yourself, write down all the reasons why you are the perfect person for the promotion and deserve to get promoted. Make sure you highlight all the strategies in this book including your top value contributions, your leadership brand, your competences, and your growth potential.

Read it before you go to sleep at night and then again first thing in the morning. Keep doing this until it sinks into the very core of your being. Once you have internalized it, it will become easier for you to advocate for yourself by stating facts about your achievement, growth potential, and leadership attributes. For example, talk about the challenges you have overcome, what you learned in the process, and what you achieved as a result.

You might feel awkward at first but the more you advocate for yourself, the easier it will get. If necessary, practice advocating for your yourself with friends and family and then with your trusted network. Remember, by becoming the best possible candidate, you have already demonstrated advocacy in action—now it is about becoming comfortable with talking about why you are the best candidate.

Once you are comfortable advocating yourself, you are ready to initiate the process of getting promoted.

1. Have the First Promotion Conversation with Your Boss

To get the ball rolling, you must talk to your boss about your desire to be promoted. Since you've done the work to become the best possible candidate, you've formed a leadership brand and you've been recognized as one of the highest-performing individuals consistently for two years or at a minimum one year with a similar rating in the works for this year. Once that's true for you, set up a meeting with your boss to have an initial conversation about your career aspirations and your desire to get promoted into a leadership role.

During this meeting, share the highlights of the work you've done to become the best possible candidate. Focus on concrete evidence that highlights your top value contributions, your growth potential, and your leadership attributes. This will prove you're ready for the next step in your career.

Next, share that you're ready to take on more responsibilities and you'd like to be considered for a promotion. With all the work you've done to become the best possible candidate, your boss should easily show support. If your boss doesn't, you need to start thinking about taking your talents elsewhere. Your boss's support is critical for you to get promoted, and if you don't feel your boss is on your team, then moving up within your organization will be incredibly difficult.

With that being said, I do hope that this conversation results in nothing but your boss's support and willingness to give constructive feedback and advice. If it does, continue your meeting by asking your boss the following questions one at a time. Stop after every question and give your boss all the time she or he needs to answer. Listen and learn. Take extensive notes, and ask clarifying questions if necessary. Show your excitement and your readiness to learn at all times.

- When do you expect there will be an opportunity for me to be considered for a promotion?
- What are the decision-making criteria?
- What is the decision-making process?
- What do I need to demonstrate in order to be considered for a promotion?
- Are there any skill gaps I need to fill?
- Who else will be the decision makers for the role?

Ask any clarifying questions you have. It's important you don't make any assumptions, and equally important you have complete clarity, especially regarding the decision-making criteria and process. There's no room for error here. Every organization, every role, and every leader does this differently, so it's imperative you understand every detail of it.

Next, ask how your boss received her or his first promotion into a leadership role. Understanding how your boss got promoted is a great way to engage your boss and understand your boss's decision-making process at a deeper level. Again, take detailed notes, as that'll help you formulate a promotion game plan after this discussion.

When your boss is done sharing the story, reiterate a specific part of the story that resonated with you and explain what you've learned from the story and will apply moving forward.

Your next step is dependent on your boss's answers to the two questions you asked earlier:

- What do I need to demonstrate in order to be considered for a promotion?
- Are there any skill gaps I need to fill?

If your boss asks you to demonstrate capabilities and/or identifies skills you need to learn, move on to Step 1(A), "Promotion-Readiness Meetings," below. If your boss doesn't identify any gaps and feels you meet all the decision-making criteria now, move on to Step 1(B), "Get Agreement to Compete."

If your boss doesn't identify any gaps and still says you can't be considered, take a breath, stay calm, and ask why in a way that invites and honors your boss's perspective. While a negative response might feel like a step in the wrong direction, don't get discouraged. This doesn't mean you won't get a promotion. Hear your boss out, and then make the best decision for you. Be sure to end the meeting by thanking your boss for being honest.

Whatever the reason—a hiring freeze, budget cuts, etc.—take the information shared with you and use it to formulate your game plan to keep working toward that promotion.

1(A). Promotion-Readiness Meetings

In this meeting (or another if you don't have time), brainstorm ways you can fill the gaps that were identified. Some questions you can ask include:

- What do I need to demonstrate to get on the top talent list (if you're not already on it)?
- Do you have any suggestions for how I can fill the gap you mentioned?

- Would external certifications or formal education help?
- Are there on-the-job trainings or training programs that the company has that you suggest I participate in?
- Are there conferences that would be helpful for me to attend?

Before the meeting is over, agree on next steps, and ask what a good cadence would be to track your progress. I'd recommend having these conversations twice a year at the very least.

At the end, thank your boss for taking the time to meet with you, and say that you'll work hard to earn your boss's support. And before the end of the day, send a thank you email to your boss summarizing your conversation and focus on what you'll demonstrate going forward in order to be considered for a leadership role.

After the meeting, immediately write down any other notes or ideas you have while the discussion is fresh in your mind. Add as priorities to your PSP any important tasks, goals, or skills you need to demonstrate and/or gaps you need to fill. Now, you'll have a weekly reminder to ensure nothing falls through the cracks.

Next, create a document titled "My Promotion-Readiness Plan" that details how you'll fill these gaps. In the plan, include specific activities and timelines that will allow you to exceed every single decision-making criterion. If there is anything you need to do to ensure the decision process flows smoothly, include that in the plan as well.

When you schedule follow-up "Promotion Readiness" meetings, use the time to:

- Share your promotion-readiness plan with your boss.
- Take your boss through the specific work you've been doing both to fill the gaps that had been identified and to exceed every decision-making criterion.
- Seek feedback on your progress.
- Ask for any other suggestions.

Continue having these promotion-readiness meetings according to the cadence you've agreed upon. Once you've demonstrated progress, and your boss agrees that you've filled the gaps as well as exceeded all the decision-making criteria, it's time to state the following to your boss: "I've been preparing for this day since our very first meeting on (insert date here) when I shared my career aspirations with you." Then continue with Step 1(B).

1(B). Get Agreement to Compete

Whether you worked through Step 1(A) or your boss confirmed you've met all the decision-making criteria after your initial conversation, you're now ready to get your boss's approval to compete for a promotion.

Start (or continue) this discussion by saying the following: "Thank you for all your guidance and support so far. I learned a lot from you and appreciate your leadership. I'm now ready to become a leader myself by taking on more responsibilities. Will you give me an opportunity to compete for the next promotional opening for (insert the specific leadership role)?"

Once your boss agrees that you'll be considered when the job is open, express thanks for your boss's time, support, trust, and confidence in you. Reiterate that this promotion is extremely important to you and that you'll work hard to earn it. Also mention that once you get the role, you'll shoulder the responsibility of a leader heavily, work very hard to become an exemplary leader, and strive to make your boss proud of the decision to consider you.

After the meeting is over, follow up with an email summarizing your conversation and say thank you again for your boss's time and support. (Putting this in writing is critical just in case you get a new boss in the middle of these conversations and you need to show what you've been promised.)

Now that your boss knows you're interested in getting promoted, know that you'll be on your boss's radar. You, your work, and your interactions will be watched more closely, so it's even more imperative that you keep executing your seven strategies in all your interactions. Consider each day as an interview for your promotion.

You might get more assignments from your boss—consider that to be a good sign even though it might temporarily increase your workload. This will be an opportunity for you to demonstrate your leadership skill of rebalancing and reprioritizing the many tasks fighting for your attention.

2. Get Support from Decision Makers and Influencers

Whether you're working hard at filling the gaps your boss identified or you're proving your promotion readiness until a position opens up for promotion, gain support from the decision makers and influencers who will be engaged in your promotion process.

It is critical that you research and make a list of the people who fall into the above categories. Know that they will have varying degrees of influence depending on who they are, and accordingly that their votes will carry the weight of their influence. Oftentimes, the higher a person is in an organization, the more influence the person carries. But sometimes a highly respected individual at a lower level can have more influence than the level implies, so don't make any assumptions. Earn the support of every decision maker and influencer by ensuring each one understands your capabilities and your potential.

How can you do this? I have a few suggestions.

First, if you already have a great relationship with certain decision makers or influencers, you can set a meeting directly and leverage all the hard work you've done to build meaningful relationships throughout your career.

If you aren't connected to them directly, go through your best relationships to determine who can introduce you to the decision makers.

232

If any of your mentors or sponsors know the decision makers, have them connect you, and if possible, recommend you.

Set up meetings with each of them with the objective to get their support. Ask for their guidance on what you need to demonstrate to be picked for the role. Listen very carefully to their answers and take extensive notes. When they're done speaking, advocate for yourself in the same way you did with your boss when you had the initial conversation about promotion. Then ask what leadership attributes they consider most important. If you already possess those attributes, mention that; and if you don't yet possess them, let them know you'll work on each of those attributes until they become part of your leadership brand.

Much like you did when speaking with your boss, thank them for their time and tell them how important this position is to you. Also write down any other notes or ideas immediately after the meeting while the discussion is fresh in your mind. And send them the same thank you email you sent to your boss, summarizing what you took away from your time together.

Each of these meetings is very critical to earn their support, as these people will be sitting around the table when you're being discussed.

3. Prepare for and Ace the Interview

Most leadership roles are extremely competitive, and the process will require one or more rounds of interviews. Once a job opens up and you're selected as a candidate for this promotion, you must prepare for your interview as if it were the most important interview of your career.

So let's work to make sure you're prepared to ace your interviews.

First, you must deeply know why you're the best possible candidate for the promotion so you can advocate for yourself. Then, write down all the reasons you're grateful to have this opportunity to compete for a leadership role. This puts you in a state of gratitude, which enhances your confidence. Regardless of the outcome of the interview, you've become worthy of a promotion, and that in and of itself is something to be grateful for.

Next, conduct mock interviews with two or three mentors and two or three leaders who are at the same level as your boss and have hired for the position you're competing for. If you can't find the right people in your organization, look for others outside your organization.

When it's time for the interview, walk into the room knowing in every ounce of your being that you are the best possible candidate and with an attitude of gratitude (instead of a sense of entitlement), which results in the highest level of confidence possible to advocate for yourself. Know that when you get that promotion, it will not only put you in the leadership pipeline; it will change the statistics of women in leadership roles! This will energize you even more and make you unbeatable. Should any limiting thoughts creep in, exercise your PQ immediately to shift your thoughts.

> **INSIGHT**
>
> **Never give up on your dream to become a leader.**

Be sure to mention why this role is important to you, and let the interviewer know that if given the opportunity to lead, you'll take this responsibility very seriously and work hard to become an exemplary leader they will be proud of.

As soon as the interview is over, thank everyone who has played a significant role in your career up to this point, including those who helped you with the interview prep. Let them know that regardless of the outcome, you would not have had the chance to compete if it were not for their help and support.

4. Accept the Results of Your Interview

If you compete and don't get a job because someone else was more qualified, so be it. The most qualified person should get the job, just as you should when you're most qualified. Don't be disheartened. Obtain feedback on what would have made you the ideal candidate, and work on those areas so you're more qualified the next time, as Seema's story illustrated in Chapter 7. Your career is a long game. Sometimes you have to try multiple times before you get the leadership position. Every time you compete for a promotion, you'll learn how to improve your future chances by applying feedback.

That being said, there are some situations that do warrant taking a deeper look at whether or not your current organization is where you should stay. Consider looking elsewhere if you experience the following:

- No concrete feedback
- A pattern of someone less qualified getting the job over you
- Multiple excellent performance reviews but no support to compete for promotions
- A promotion in name only with no added responsibility or the right compensation as you read in Sangeeta's story in Chapter 4

If you do choose to leave, remember that you've built relevant and marketable skills and worked hard to become the best possible candidate for your desired promotion. This means you absolutely can get promoted elsewhere. Use connectors to meet people outside your organization, and remember there are plenty of headhunters willing to do the work for high-potential candidates like you. Don't let anything get in the way of your leadership promotion. You can change plans but keep alive your desire to get promoted.

5. Celebrate Your Promotion

When you get promoted to a leadership role—and you will—celebrate yourself before anything else! You worked really hard and made it here, so celebrate in a big way. Go on a vacation, treat yourself to something you wouldn't normally buy for yourself, or donate more generously than you have before to your favorite charity.

Reflect upon your journey that brought you to this defining moment in your career, recognize all your effort, and be grateful that you have this opportunity to lead as leadership is a privilege. Let your success sink into every ounce of your being.

Once you start your new position, aim to become the leader you wish you had. Work hard to own the added responsibility you gained, not just for your success, but for your team's as well. Your every action and decision has an amplified effect. Become aware of this very intensely, and shoulder this responsibility heavily.

Also be aware that you'll likely be a topic of discussion at your employees' dinner tables, and how you treat them will be discussed with their family and friends. Your kindness and compassion during any time of need for your employees will be remembered long after your career is over. So work hard to ensure that those who work for you respect and admire you as a leader, and strive to be someone that the people on your team want to follow and know has their backs.

> **INSIGHT**
>
> Celebrate and honor your achievements.

Bear in mind, too, that as a leader, you'll engage in hiring, identifying high-potential employees, and influencing policies for your company. Become intentional about representing other women and be an advocate for them.

Also remember as a woman in a leadership position, other women will be watching you. Strive to become a role model for them, and you will become their inspiration. Become intentional about representing other women and become an advocate for them. Once you settle into your new role, reach out to some high-potential women to mentor them to help them become leaders, too!

Don't forget to redefine your short- and long-term definitions of success when you get promoted. Come back to this book and continue to apply the strategies to keep rising higher. You will have evolved and you will see things differently. Remember, this process is ongoing and you should keep working until you reach your full leadership potential!

Your impact, influence, and ability to create a rising tide that lifts more women will keep growing as you rise higher and higher up the leadership ladder. When we women support each other at every rung of the leadership ladder, we can change the world of business forever. Together we will become the change our world needs. There will be no more "broken rungs," and we will achieve gender parity at *all* leadership levels. We will be in every room where decisions are made. There will be no negative stereotypes and gender biases. You are a part of the change you want to see in our world.

SET YOUR INTENTIONS

Promise yourself:

- I will become intentional about getting promoted regardless of what level I'm at.
- I will realize my maximum leadership potential and never drop off the leadership pipeline.
- I will become the change agent for achieving gender parity at all leadership levels.

EPILOGUE

INTENTIONALLY PAY IT FORWARD AND LIFT OTHER WOMEN

When you have worked hard, and done
well, and done, and walked through that doorway of
opportunity, you do not slam it shut behind you.
You reach back, and you give other folks the
same chances that helped you succeed.

MICHELLE OBAMA

WHEN I look back at my career and my life, the moments of success that I felt when I was an instrument in helping someone else achieve success weighed more heavily than anything I'd achieved for myself. This is why the above quote by Michelle Obama resonates with me at my core, and that's what we'll be talking about now: how as a leader you can intentionally lift other women.

At the beginning of 2014, a little over two years after I started in my position as a vice president, I had achieved my long-term definition of success. I started reflecting and thinking about what my next long-term definition of success should be. I defined it as pay back to the universe for all the opportunities that were given to me.

Yes, I worked hard to seize those opportunities, but I've also always been acutely aware of how many other women work harder than I do and are not given the opportunities I got.

Just as I made my decision, the universe gave me one of my finest gifts: time with my mom. In May 2014, she came to visit us from Tanzania. In July 2014, I left IBM to pursue my new definition of success, and as a result, I got to spend time with my mom, whose health was starting to deteriorate.

On October 18, we celebrated my mom's seventy-fifth birthday at my house, and in her honor, I cooked chicken biryani for all the guests. She traveled back to Tanzania on November 8, and her health got worse shortly after. In February 2015, upon further testing, we learned that she had stage 4 GI tract cancer, and it had spread through her body. I spent the last few weeks of her life with her in Tanzania and was holding her hands in prayer as she took her last breath on March 12, 2015.

Spending time with my mom in Tanzania impacted me deeply in three profound ways. First, it made me even more aware of how far I'd come from my humble beginnings and made me even more grateful for the opportunities I'd been given. Second, it made me recognize how deeply she inspired me to achieve success. And finally, I realized what will matter in the end is not the success I achieved but the success I help others achieve.

A little over a month later, on April 17, 2015, I was invited to be a keynote speaker at my alma mater, University of Wisconsin–La Crosse, for a conference called "Women Moving Ahead," which was inspired by Sheryl Sandberg's book *Lean In*. In preparation for this talk, I reflected deeply upon my entire career journey so I could share poignant insights that would enable the more than 400 women in the audience to move ahead in their own journeys.

The energy, excitement, hugs, tears, and testimonials of hope that came after my talk made me feel more successful than I ever had before. And those stories of possibility and hope inspired me that day to become an empowerment speaker. Since then, I've spoken to thousands of women globally to help them accelerate their career success and emerge as leaders. I also continued to mentor more women.

I share these stories with you to help you understand what happens when you intentionally start lifting other women. Not only could you change the lives of the women you help, but doing so will not only make you feel enormously successful, it will also fill you with a deep sense of gratitude and appreciation for all you've got.

There are many ways to lift other women. For example, if this book helps your career, share your experiences with other women so those experiences can help them as well. What you share will become a page in their story, and they'll in turn share experiences that will become a page in the story of others.

Leadership is a responsibility, a gift, and an opportunity that can create a rippling impact you'll never be able to measure, as it can last generations. Once you get a title of a leader, your influence and impact will extend to far more women than you likely ever imagined.

No matter where you are in your career journey, remember that other women in your community, your extended family, your company, and other companies are watching and learning from you. So, first and foremost, be intentional about what you're modeling for them. No longer is your brand just about you, but it's also a brand for other women to emulate. It can also become a measure of others that look like you. Always be aware of this enormous responsibility. It will give you the strength to face difficult situations because you're in this not just for yourself now, but for others that you represent as well.

Your mere presence can inspire countless women. Your words will weigh heavy and can inspire other women to reach their maximum leadership potential. Set a high standard of excellence for yourself so you may shine as bright as possible. Your brightness will inspire everyone you interact with to also shine.

You've made many promises to yourself to ensure you stay in the leadership pipeline and emerge as a leader. Now, I'd like to ask you to make three more promises so not only can we collectively achieve gender parity in leadership roles but we can also lift other women by paying forward:

- I promise to reach back and give other women the same chances that helped me succeed.
- I promise to intentionally use my time, talent, and treasure to uplift other women.
- I promise to intentionally engage in discussions and decisions that pave the way to lift other women.

I'm excited about the possibility of what we can achieve together. I would like to end my book with my favorite Rumi quote, "Every moment I shape my destiny with a chisel, I am a carpenter of my own soul."

Chisel intentionally!

THE 8 INTENTIONAL STRATEGIES TO SHOW YOUR WORTH

1 INTENTIONAL SUCCESS

2 INTENTIONAL ATTENTION

3 INTENTIONAL WORK-LIFE BALANCE

4 INTENTIONAL VALUE CREATION

5 INTENTIONAL GROWTH

6 INTENTIONAL RELATIONSHIPS

7 INTENTIONAL LEADERSHIP BRANDING

8 INTENTIONAL PROMOTION

INDEX

ABOUT THE AUTHOR

 **Shelmina Babai Abji** is an author, board member, speaker, former IBM VP, angel investor, and distinguished alumni who is devoted to creating gender equality in leadership by helping career women emerge as leaders.

Shelmina started her journey with humble beginnings in Tanzania. Driven by her desire to lift herself and her family out of poverty, she left home at the age of 15 to pursue higher education.

When she started her career, she was an underrepresented woman in the male-dominated field of technology. She was also under-educated as compared to others, underprivileged in her economic status, and under-proficient in the language and culture.

She learned many lessons and went from being the first college graduate in her family to becoming one of the highest-ranking women of color at IBM while raising her two children as a single mother since they were 4 and 2.

She has led global teams and various businesses in multiple sectors. She has delivered over $1 billion in revenues annually and has consistently maintained high client satisfaction as well as team morale. She was a decision maker in hiring and promoting hundreds of professionals. At the peak of her career, she left IBM to pursue her passion for creating gender equality in leadership.

Shelmina now speaks at corporations, colleges, and conferences globally. She has mentored hundreds of women and impacted the careers of thousands. She also serves on the advisory board of Girl Up, a global leadership development initiative positioning girls to be leaders in the movement for gender equality. She previously served on the board of TiE-Seattle, Bellevue College, and Young Women Empowered.

Shelmina has degrees in computer science from the University of Wisconsin–La Crosse, and mathematics from Wadia College in Pune, India. As part of IBM's top talent, she received extensive leadership training at IBM and Harvard.

NOTES

NOTES